THE NATURE OF THE TOWPATH

A NATURAL HISTORY GUIDE TO THE OHIO & ERIE CANAL TOWPATH TRAIL   BY PEG & ROB BOBEL

Printed in the United States of America.

ISBN 0-9630416-2-2

Made possible by grants from
The George Gund Foundation
and Eastern National

CONTENTS

LOCATOR MAPS

The Ohio & Erie Canal Towpath Trail
is located within Cuyahoga Valley National
Recreation Area, a 33,000 acre unit of
the National Park System.

For more information write to:

Superintendent
Cuyahoga Valley National Recreation Area
15610 Vaughn Road
Brecksville, Ohio 44141-3018
216-524-1497
www.nps.gov/cuva

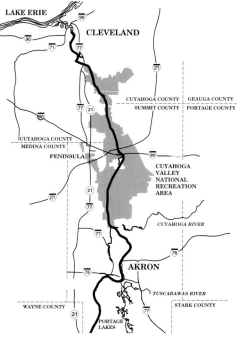

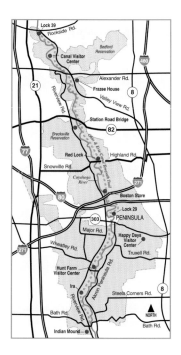

You need only sit still long enough in some
attractive spot in the woods that
all its inhabitants may exhibit themselves
to you by turns.

Henry David Thoreau

INTRODUCTION

People shape the places where they live. They plant trees and they cut trees. They build ponds and they dig wells. They tramp paths and construct roads. In the Cuyahoga River valley, native Americans, pioneers, mule drivers, and farmers all shaped the land. They have been a part of the valley's natural history story, affecting and being affected by all that makes up the nature of the valley. Today you, like others before you, will change and be changed by this place, to one degree or another. This guide is for you and other modern day explorers visiting the same valley that pioneers from New England found so enticing.

It is for visitors to the valley who are looking for a deeper understanding and appreciation of how people and natural events in the past shaped what we see and experience today. This guide is for those who want to know this place better—why it looks as it does, what lives here, and how nature fits it all together.

When pioneers like David Hudson and Jonathan Hale and their families came to this valley, they came as settlers, not explorers. They were determined to make a new life here in the Western Reserve wilderness. They put down roots and set in motion forces that helped guide subsequent settlement and sculpting of the land. Later settlers conceived and built the canal which altered the landscape in an even more dramatic and lasting way. And in the course of their settlement and farming, and the commercial and industrial development that followed, the landscape and native flora and fauna were affected in ways that we can detect today.

The Cuyahoga River valley now is at a point in its history where places that had been tamed are now reverting to wildness. In some places, old scars are healing. In others, land managers are attempting to strike a balance between preserving the historic scene while protecting natural habitats.

The following pages introduce you to the nature of one of the most significant trails in the valley, both for its history and its proximity to natural areas. Here you will meet the plants and animals which share the area surrounding the 19.7 miles of the Ohio & Erie Canal Towpath Trail in Cuyahoga Valley National Recreation Area (CVNRA). Since its completion in 1993, the Towpath Trail has become one of the most popular recreational trails in northeast Ohio. Although many people come strictly to exercise, others come to the trail to delve deeper into this diverse and interesting place.

This guide can lead you beyond the obvious, towards a fuller understanding of the nature of the Towpath Trail. It's like the difference between walking alone or with a young child. With a child along, you find yourself moving at a slower pace. You'll be asked about the woolly bear squiggling across the trail, you'll notice the ankle-high wildflower, and you'll share the discovery of a robin's nest. This guide can be that child with you—asking you to slow down, look around, pay attention, ask questions.

The Ohio & Erie Canal Towpath Trail follows the route of the historic Ohio & Erie Canal towpath—the path that the mules and drivers followed, hauling canal boats by towlines. The trail is located on the historic towpath itself except in a few places where the original towpath is eroded away. The historic canal extended from Portsmouth on the Ohio River to Cleveland on Lake Erie. In November of 1996, the Ohio & Erie Canal National Heritage Corridor was established between Cleveland and Zoar in recognition of the significance the canal played in this region's history. This designation encouraged park districts in the corridor to develop other sections of the towpath for recreational use, with a long-range plan of connecting Cleveland to Zoar by

1902

State Boat #1 just south of Stone Road

trail once again. Although this guide describes only the Towpath Trail within the boundary of CVNRA (Rockside Road in Cuyahoga County to Bath Road in Summit County), it can be useful when visiting other portions of the towpath in the corridor because much of the flora and fauna is similar.

This guide is divided into eight sections. Each section follows a theme that will help you understand how human history has affected the landscape and ecology of the valley or how natural processes are at work today. The introduction of each section helps explain why certain combinations of

particularly interesting. In this way, you will become acquainted with many, but not all, of the species found along the trail. Please view this guide as a hostess at a large party who takes

you to meet a few of the common and interesting characters, but never attempts to have you meet everyone. You'll leave knowing a few new characters, yet interested in returning to meet and learn about others.

plants and animals are found together and how these communities of life relate to the geography and history of the trail. The text then describes plants and animals which are typical in the area or

Some species in this guide can be found throughout the valley and others are more localized. Each section highlights certain plants and animals that are likely to be found there, but many of these can also be found elsewhere along the trail. Of all the trails in CVNRA, the Towpath Trail offers an especially good introduction to the wildlife of the park because it passes through a variety of habitats, including several wetlands. By the time you have completed the entire trail, in all seasons and at various times of the day, you will have learned many of the species found in the Cuyahoga valley.

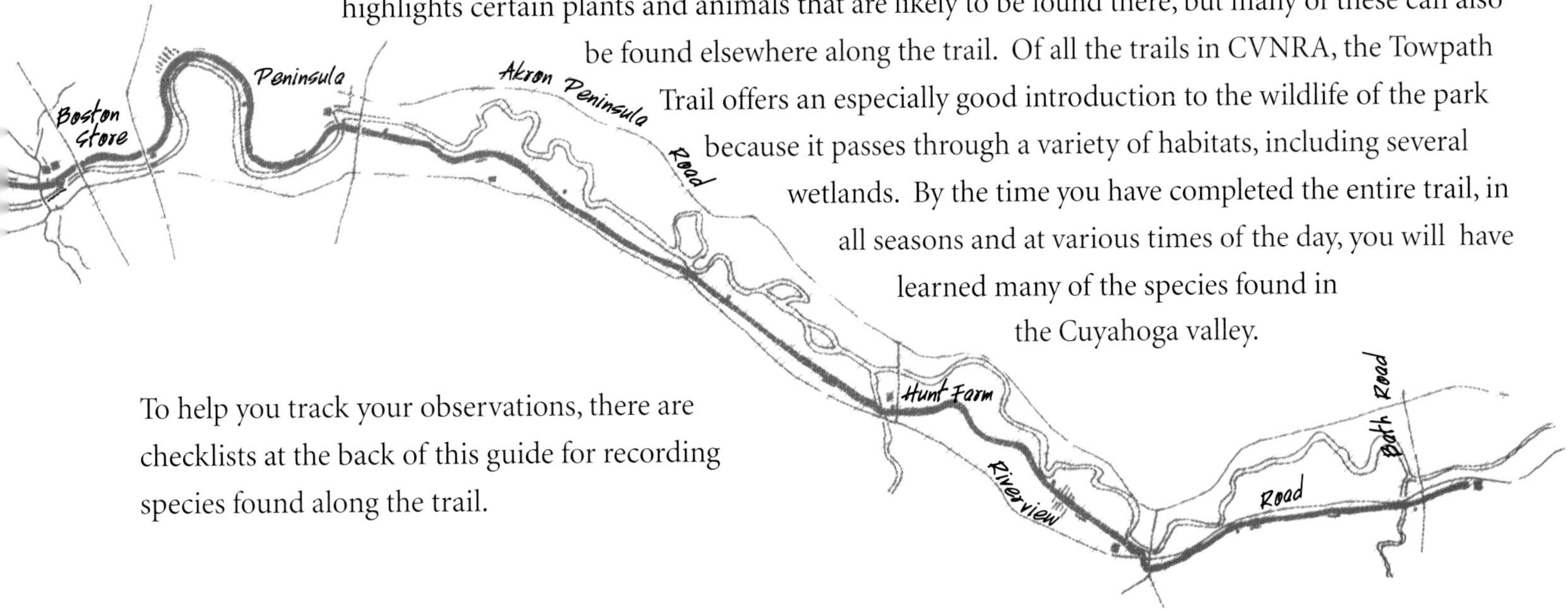

To help you track your observations, there are checklists at the back of this guide for recording species found along the trail.

Boston Store

Peninsula

Akron Peninsula Road

Hunt Farm

Riverview Road

Road

Bath Road

Common names are used in the text, but the checklists include scientific names since common names can change and differ widely from region to region. These lists include only the species found in the areas reached by the Towpath Trail, while the larger CVNRA is home to additional species not listed here. It is hoped that this guide might lead you to explore more of the recreation area.

Taking along a few items in a daypack can help you get the most out of your outing—a water bottle, hand lens, field guides, binoculars, notebook, pencil can all be helpful. But don't worry if you don't own all these items—the CVNRA visitor centers have Discovery Packs for your use. Each pack includes binoculars, magnifying glasses, field guides, an activity book, a discovery journal, and other supplies and equipment. You can use the pack for a nominal fee, and the discovery journal is yours to keep. These packs are especially designed for families, home schoolers, and scout groups. You can also take advantage of ranger-led programs on the trail to extend your experiences and knowledge. But the only truly essential item to take along is attention. You will see the most by going slowly and using all your senses. Sitting down is even better.

Benches along the trail allow you to sit in comfort while nature comes to you. If you're cycling, choose a spot or two to stop, get off your bike, and simply observe.

Before going out on the trail, you might want to read an entire section of this guide. Fixing a picture of something in your mind helps you to see it. You may surprise yourself at seeing things where you never noticed them before. Make notes or sketches of unfamiliar plants or animals so that you can look them up later. While on the trail, relax, be patient, let nature come. Some days will yield more than others. The best naturalists have their lean days when all seems to be hiding. A lean day is just an invitation to return another time.

To some of you the Towpath Trail is already a familiar place, to others it is brand new. May you all, regardless of your experience on the trail, come to see with new eyes, new appreciation, new enjoyment, and may you truly get to know this place and your role in it, and become part of the Nature of the Towpath Trail.

For A Safe and Pleasant Trip

This is a shared trail for walkers, joggers, bicyclists, equestrians, and those using wheelchairs.
• Keep to the right except to pass
• Give a clear warning before passing
• Keep pets on a 6-foot leash
• Move completely off the trail when stopped

To those who have not yet learned the secret of
true happiness, begin now to study the little
things in your own door yard

George Washington Carver

LAND OF
FIRST QUALITY

Lock 39 Trailhead on Rockside Road and the historic Frazee House near Sagamore Road mark the north and south ends of this section of the Ohio & Erie Canal Towpath Trail. For 3 3/4 miles the trail parallels Canal Road. The road, the canal, and the towpath are all relatively straight, constructed routes in contrast to the nearby Cuyahoga River's naturally meandering route. The trail offers an exceptional vantage point from which to observe, experience, and understand how the river works its way through the valley and what goes on in the adjoining fields, the strips of woods, and the pond-like canal.

Lock 39 Road

P Rockside

Mile 11

Canal

Pilgeruh

Cuyahoga

Road

Mile 12

N

P

Lock 38

River

Canal Visitor Center

Tinkers Creek

Mile 13

Pleasant Valley Road

Mile 14

Lock 31

Frazee House

12

Recorded history tells us what this area may have looked like hundreds of years ago. Somewhere here along the river, in 1786, a group of Native Americans and Moravian missionaries stopped to build a temporary community on their way back to the Tuscarawas River valley. As they reported,

"We came early to an old town, inhabited formerly by the Ottawas, which was the first place we had come upon where we could remain, for up to this point from the mouth of the river there is nothing but wild forest. . ."
It already being mid-June, they resolved to set up camp here and plant corn and vegetables *"where it appeared there was formerly an Indian corn field."* This stopping place came to be called Pilgerruh, or Pilgrims' Rest.

Ten years later, missionary John Heckewelder

described the river valley to a friend, commenting on the clarity of the river and stating *"there is a great deal of Land of first Quality on this River."* He goes on to describe the "rich Bottoms" as having timber of *"Black Walnut, or White Thorn Trees, intermixed with various other Trees as Cherry, Mulberry, &c The ground entirely covered with high Nettles."*

In other bottom land areas he noted *"lofty Oaks, Poplar, or Tulip tree, Elm, Hickory, Sugar Maple yet intermixed with Black Walnut, Cherry, Mulberry, Grape Vines, White Thorn, Haw-bush &c &c Ash &c. Wild Hops of an excellent quality grow also plentifully on this River. . .The Cujahaga Country abounds in Game, such as Elk, Deer, Turkey, Raccoons &c. . ."*

13

Over the succeeding two hundred years, descendants and new emigrants expanded the early settlers' farming. The cultivated fields replaced much of the bottom land forest. When the canal was built in the 1820s, it brought other changes to the landscape and nature of the valley. Of the many changes, two are significant to note here. The canal altered the local topography and drainage patterns, creating in effect a long pond of sluggish water, and the increased settlement brought the seeds of alien plant species via the canal.

Lock 31 at Wilson's Mill c. 1890

Today there is much to see here along the Towpath Trail. Cultivated crops interspersed with patches of forest and fields create a tapestry of native and introduced plant species which provide food, shelter, and nesting sites for various animals. Along the trail during the late summer months, 6 to 7- foot tall purple-flowered ironweed and the daisy-like wingstem thrive in the shade of the big willows, sycamores, and cottonwoods. Woodpeckers seek out insects and find nesting holes in hollow places in the larger trees. Bordering the canal, shrubby staghorn sumacs retain their red fruit throughout the year. In warm seasons green frogs leap out of sight into the safety of the water as you approach, and white tail dragonflies hunt over the still water for mosquito meals. You may want to return again and again to acquaint yourself with the colorful mixture of plants and animals which now share this "land of first quality."

Birds

The prevalent birds of this section are large, easy to identify, and indicative of a mostly agricultural landscape. Gulls, Canada geese, rock doves, and starlings can be found any time during the year, while the presence or absence of turkey vultures announce the arrival of spring or the coming of winter. Before 1950 Canada geese came here only as migrants or winter visitors. In the 1950s and 1960s the Ohio Department of Natural Resources established refuges for geese in various areas in the state. The geese adapted well and by 1988 were considered abundant nesters. Geese appear by the thousands in late fall, making them most numerous throughout the winter months. In February and March many of these can be seen overhead in V-shaped flocks, heading for Canada to nest. Those which remain nest almost anywhere along the canal and river, forming ground nests from grass, reeds, and leaves. A pair will mate for life and raise an annual brood of olive-yellow goslings. Geese can be quite protective of their nest and goslings and may vie for the right-of-way along the trail!

The occasional gull seen during most of the year in the valley is the ring-billed gull, but in winter large numbers of ring-billed and herring

Canada Goose

gulls can be seen flying low over the Cuyahoga River in search of food. They come inland from Lake Erie (only 14 miles away by air) during the day to feed in the open water of the river, then at dusk return to the lake. Gulls are scavengers, filling an important role in nature, "cleaning up" by consuming dead fish, rodents, grasshoppers, and human garbage.

Turkey Vulture

Starlings and rock doves, or pigeons, are often seen around Wilson's Feed Mill. Both birds were introduced to America from Europe. The iridescent starlings were brought from England in 1890 to introduce "Shakespeare's birds" to the New World. By 1960 there were over 50 million starlings through-

Red-Tail Hawk

out the United States. They are a serious threat to our native cavity nesters such as bluebirds, as they aggressively compete for available nest holes. The rock doves prefer cities apparently because they resemble the rocky cliffs where they ancestrally nested. They eat grains and seeds of grasses and weeds.

Turkey vultures, or buzzards, return to northern Ohio about the same time every year, in

mid-March. These large birds soar effortlessly and are easy to identify in flight because they teeter and hold their wings in a distinct V-shape, or dihedral. They, like gulls, are valuable scavengers, consuming mostly carrion which they locate both by sight and smell.

Flowers

The most notable flowers of this section are large, easy to spot summer plants: green-headed coneflower, cow parsnip, tall ironweed, lance-leaved goldenrod, and common teasel. The shortest of these is the goldenrod, 2 to 4 feet tall, while the cow parsnip can grow to 10 feet. The cow parsnip's broad clusters of white flowers are carried atop a thick, woolly stem.

Common Teasel

The huge plants are unmistakable, rising above all others in a field.

The extremely prickly teasels are native to Asia and Europe. The beautifully colored blue to purple flowers mature first in the middle of the spike then spread up and down. One of the more interesting and obvious plants growing just south of Canal Visitor Center is poison hemlock. Many visitors stop to admire these tall white-flowered plants growing in large expanses between the towpath and the river. This nonnative perennial in the Parsley family grows 5 to 6 feet tall. You can recognize it by its smooth, spotted stem, finely divided leaves (resembling parsley), and tiny white flowers in umbels (umbrella-like clusters). Its poisonous properties have been known for hundreds of years and may be the hemlock Socrates drank.

Trees

Although farm fields have largely replaced the bottom land forests, native trees such as black cherry and elm still grow in the river valley as they did in the days of pioneer settlement. The largest trees are cottonwoods, willows, and sycamores, all favoring the wet edges of the river. The

Box Elder Keys

box elder, also known as ashleaf maple, is also common along the river and canal. Certain characteristics make this tree easy to identify: it has a short trunk, usually somewhat deformed with many stump sprouts, a maple-like leaf, and seeds in paired, winged structures called keys. These remain conspicuously attached all winter long.

Mammals

White-tailed deer, prevalent throughout the valley, prefer this type of habitat of scrubby old fields. They feed on the leaves, buds, and tender new shoots of trees and other succulent vegetation. Watch for them browsing in the fields or seeking cover in the wooded borders along the river. Evidence of beaver and muskrat can be found along the river and canal. Look for tree chews and stick lodges of the beaver, and feeding platforms and feeding shelters of the muskrats.

Insects

Field crickets liven up any summertime excursion near fields or pastures. Their familiar song is a series of triple chirps. Another insect of the fields is the Carolina locust. Being the color of dry soil, it's difficult to spot until it takes flight, making a purring or fluttering sound. Red-legged grasshoppers are dark brown with, unsurprisingly, red hind legs. Their eggs, like those of the field cricket, are deposited in the ground and overwinter. The nymphs appear in the spring and by summer mature into adults. The music-making of male grasshoppers and crickets serves several purposes: as a warning, an announcemenof territory, and as a part of courtship.

The scarlet-and-green leafhopper distinguishes itself by its tiny size and brilliant coloring. Forewings are orange to red, edged in green or blue with a diagonal stripe forming a deep V when the wings are folded. Aptly named, leafhoppers are agile jumpers.

Reptiles

The northern water snake, pictured above, is the most frequently sighted snake along the Towpath Trail. It is active during the day and night and spends its entire life near or in the water. During the day you might see it basking on rocky ledges and the sandstone canal locks. Young snakes are often brightly banded showing red crescents, while older snakes tend to turn a uniform dark brown or black. The markings of this snake resemble the water moccasin, found in the southern United States, ***however there are <u>no</u> venomous snakes in Cuyahoga Valley National Recreation Area.*** The northern water snake feeds on a variety of aquatic animals, mainly frogs and fish. The snake is an excellent swimmer, often catching its meal underwater. It frequently eats unhealthy animals, helping to maintain a well balanced aquatic ecosystem.

Amphibians

Amphibians include salamanders, frogs, and toads, and are defined as vertebrates which usually begin life in the water as tadpoles with gills, later developing lungs and living on land. The two amphibians most likely seen in this section of trail are the American toad and green frog, both found throughout the valley. Unless you are especially sharp-eyed, green frogs sense your presence before you spot them. When not in the water, they stay within jumping distance and as you approach

they give themselves away by letting out a "wheep!" while leaping into the water. In early summer a female green frog lays up to 5,000 eggs. The eggs hatch quickly in three to seven days, then live as tadpoles from 3 to 22 months before metamorphosing into mature frogs.

Winter

The quiet and relative emptiness of winter allows you to explore the more subtle signs of life along the canal. And in

Queen Anne's Lace
root & rosette

spite of freezing cold, not all greenery is gone from the fields. Some of the field plants are winter annuals: the seeds which drop in late summer germinate immediately then spend the winter as rosettes. Biennials spend one full year as rosettes. Some of the rosettes in the fields are common burdock, evening primrose, and Queen Anne's lace, or wild carrot. The wild carrot rosette is easily recognizable, looking exactly like a carrot top.

Topography

The Cuyahoga River itself has been slowly and persistently changing this landscape. There are good places along the trail to

19

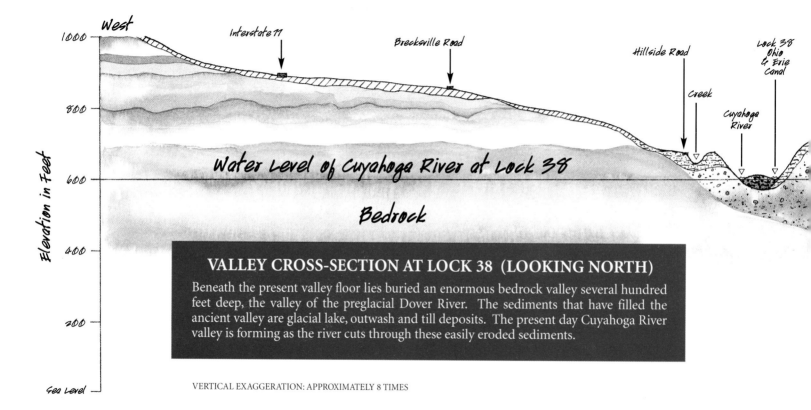

West

1000

Interstate 77

Brecksville Road

Hillside Road

Lock 38
Ohio
& Erie
Canal

Creek

Cuyahoga
River

800

Water Level of Cuyahoga River at Lock 38

600

Elevation in Feet

Bedrock

400

200

Sea Level

VALLEY CROSS-SECTION AT LOCK 38 (LOOKING NORTH)

Beneath the present valley floor lies buried an enormous bedrock valley several hundred feet deep, the valley of the preglacial Dover River. The sediments that have filled the ancient valley are glacial lake, outwash and till deposits. The present day Cuyahoga River valley is forming as the river cuts through these easily eroded sediments.

VERTICAL EXAGGERATION: APPROXIMATELY 8 TIMES

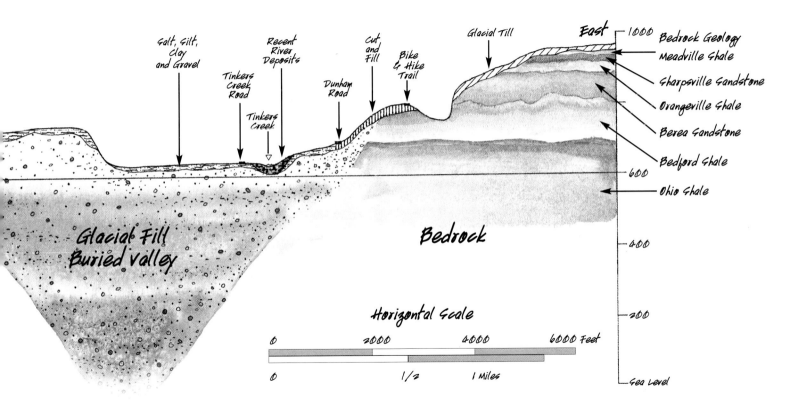

Horizontal Scale

observe the Cuyahoga River at work. As it winds back and forth, it comes close to the trail then moves almost out of sight, outlined in the distance by a narrow band of trees along its banks. Just as the river is always there, but sometimes out of sight, so too its energy is always there, invisibly working the banks and carrying its load of sediment.

The Cuyahoga River works its way along a rather shallow slope toward Lake Erie and ultimately, the Atlantic Ocean. (Just a few miles south of here, the streams flow south to the Ohio and Mississippi Rivers on their way to the Gulf of Mexico.) The valley side walls are relatively steep, but the slope along the length of the valley is very gentle. The slope of the river itself, called the channel slope, is shallower yet as it winds back and forth across the valley. If you were to stretch the river out, you would find it drops only seven feet per mile.

The result of this shallow gradient is a process called meandering. Sinuously carving through the land, the river's energy is channeled more outward than downward, eroding into banks rather than down into the bottom. The meandering river creates a flood plain, the level land on either side of the river where the river periodically stores excess water and deposits silt, creating the fertile areas so prized for farming.

Vertical, or cut, banks along the river generally indicate active erosion, usually on the outside of a meander. More gently sloped gravel banks, or point bars, are usually found on the inside of a meander.

Red-stemmed Japanese knotweed, a nonnative plant, spreads rapidly on newly exposed riverbanks.

A river is the most human and companionable of all inanimate things. It has a life, a character, a voice of its own, and is as full of good fellowship as a sugar-maple is of sap.

Henry Van Dyke

THE NARROWS

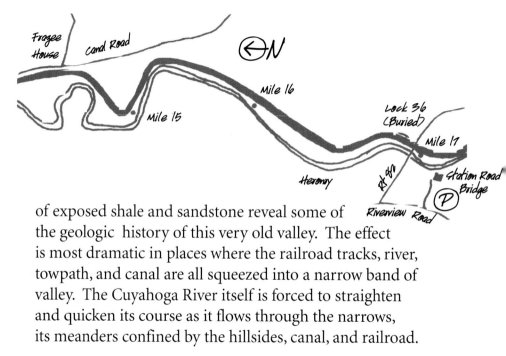

Between Canal Road and Station Road, the Ohio and Erie Canal Towpath Trail provides entry into a unique region of the Cuyahoga River valley. Nowhere else in Cuyahoga Valley National Recreation Area is the valley floor as narrow as it is in the 2 1/2 miles of the Pinery Narrows. At Lock 36 in the narrows, the valley floor width is only 400 feet, compared to a width of 3,045 feet at Lock 37, the next lock north, near Wilson's Feed Mill. At times in the narrows you are just a stone's throw from the east valley wall, where layers of exposed shale and sandstone reveal some of the geologic history of this very old valley. The effect is most dramatic in places where the railroad tracks, river, towpath, and canal are all squeezed into a narrow band of valley. The Cuyahoga River itself is forced to straighten and quicken its course as it flows through the narrows, its meanders confined by the hillsides, canal, and railroad.

South end of Pinery Narrows, Lock 36 c. 1890

Entering the Pinery Narrows you leave the roads and road noises behind. Legs, spoked wheels, a canoe, or a locomotive are the only entrees into this region. Local history tells us that this area came to be called Pinery Narrows because of the many white pines that once grew here. In the 1800s they were cut, and the straight, 80 to 100-foot trunks were floated to Lake Erie to become the masts of Great Lakes' sailing ships. Now that the area is no longer timbered, a mixture of hardwoods, pines, and hemlocks have revegetated the steep slopes of the narrows.

In the narrows and for 17 miles north of here, the canal still carries water as it did when the canal was being used for transportation. Use of the canal ceased after the great flood of 1913, however steel factories to the north found the canal useful as a reliable source of cooling water. The canal has been maintained and watered for that use for most of this century. The Towpath Trail winds between the more sluggish water of the canal and the faster, more oxygenated water of the river. Different plants and animals find the two types of water habitat hospitable. To one side you might find a pair of mallards resting on the slowly moving canal water, while to the other side you might sight a kingfisher perched at the tip of a sycamore limb, eyeing the swift water below for a fish dinner.

The trail's proximity to the river makes this a good place to investigate riparian or stream side habitat. The sycamores and box elders along the river's banks are important not only because they provide habitat for land animals, but also because they are critical to the health of the river and its aquatic inhabitants. Tree roots help stabilize the banks, lessening the amount of silt which enters the river. The roots and fallen trees provide protective cover for fish, crayfish, and aquatic insects. Leaves and other plant matter that fall into the water constitute the primary food for many aquatic organisms. The shade keeps the water cooler, allowing it to hold more oxygen, vital to certain insects and fish.

In between the river and the canal, where the valley widens slightly, the land was cleared to squeeze in a few farm fields, taking advantage of the rich floodplain soils. Farmers turned the canal towpath into a farm lane to reach their fields. Today you will find that the edges of the cultivated fields host plant species such as foxtail grass, curled dock, and pokeweed, all plants that first take hold in disturbed soils. They are nonnative species, brought to America from Europe, but now so common that it is hard to imagine the landscape without them. Here goldfinches dart about the thistle patches, and cabbage butterflies cruise the fields for cabbage-like plants. All through the Pinery Narrows you can explore the fast lane of the river, the slow lane of the canal, and the spacious butterfly-filled fields in between.

27

Eastern Cottonwood   Coyote   Box Elder   Black Rat Snake   Thistle

Riparian Habitat

American Goldfinch   Great Blue Heron   Woodchuck   Damselfly   Sycamore

Birds

Perhaps the most magnificent bird you are likely to see in this area is the great blue heron. Herons nest and roost in colonies called heronries. There is a large heronry located deep in the narrows on the west side of the river, visible from the trail when the leaves are off the trees. There are over 100 stick nests built high in the trees. The great blue is the largest heron in the United States and is unmistakable, flying over the river with slow, steady wing beats, head crooked back and long legs trailing, or standing motionless in shallow water, stalking a fish or frog. The herons' appearance and guttural voice evoke images of prehistoric pterodactyl days.

In contrast to the 4-foot tall heron, the tiny ruby-throated hummingbird is less than

Great Blue Heron

4 inches long. Of the sixteen humming-birds found in the United States, the ruby-throated is the only one regularly found in the east. Look for it hovering among jewelweed and other flowering plants, eating both insects and nectar. Hummingbirds are the only birds that can fly backward.

Summer

The bright yellow male American goldfinch can be seen in the weedy thistle fields in the spring and summer. This bird nests later than most, waiting for the thistle to ripen. Goldfinches use the thistledown to line their nests and the seeds to feed their young.

Winter

Their cheerful "perchicoree" call and undulating flight are other clues to their identity. A year-round resident, the goldfinch turns a drab olive color in the winter.

Five species of woodpeckers frequent the towpath areas. Each species has a distinctive call and its own rhythm of drumming. One of them, the red-bellied woodpecker, announces itself with a loud "churr-churr." Its name seems confusing—it has only a soft wash of color on its belly, but a bright red crown.

Flowers

Bristly burdocks and prickly thistles thrive in the unshaded old fields and at the edges of cultivated fields. Both plants grow vigorously, aggressively spreading throughout an unplowed field. Common burdock is a native of Europe, as are most of the thistle species. The fruits, or burs, of the burdock which readily stick tight to clothing or animal fur, and the sharp spines of the thistles cause most hikers to find them less than friendly.

Common Burdock

Nonetheless, burdocks and thistles have their merits: burdocks yield good greens and edible roots, and thistles attract many species of butterflies.

Other field plants include curled dock, pokeweed, and goldenrod. Wingstem and jewelweed grow along the shady margins of the trail.

Trees

Two tree species are noteworthy in the Pinery Narrows. The first is the namesake for the area, the white pine. White pine wood was perfect for masting ships—light and yet strong—and the lightness of the wood made it easy to float to the mills. The trees were highly valued for other

31

White pines and eastern hemlocks green the valley year-round, as they have done for thousands of years. They are native to this region, whereas spruces and other evergreens were introduced. The needles and cones of white pines and hemlocks help in their identification. White pine needles are 2-4 inches long and are in bundles of five. Slender, 3-10 inch long cones hang from the pine branches. Hemlocks have half-inch, flat needles, marked with two white lines on their undersides, and inch-long, pendant cones with relatively few scales. Hemlocks are a dominant tree species in the community of plants found in cool creek ravines. White pines prefer well-drained, sandy soils.

Eastern Hemlock

White Pine

pioneer uses as well: covered bridges, houses, shingles, looms, and furniture were all made of white pine. Now the white pines are again growing in the narrows on the slopes above the canal. At a distance, a white pine can be recognized by its pagoda shape and whorled branches which grow in separated tiers up the perfectly straight trunk. Up close, you can identify the tree by the needles which are thin, soft, 3 to 5 inches long, and in clusters of five.

Down along the river, well adapted to the wet soil of the lowlands, sycamore trees tower above most other species. They too can be recognized at a long distance. These trees with mottled cream, tan, and green bark beautifully outline the streams and rivers along which they grow, standing out from among dark-trunked species.

Sycamores grow to a larger trunk diameter than any other native deciduous tree.

Chimney swifts used to roost in large hollow sycamore trunks before there were chimneys to roost in. Sycamores produce an unusual looking fruit, a round ball that hangs on the tree through winter then falls and fluffs apart, widely distributing its seeds. The round brown fruits give the tree its other common name, buttonwood.

Sycamore

Mammals

White-tailed deer, beaver, and groundhogs can all be seen along this section of the Towpath Trail. Groundhogs or woodchucks usually live in the meadows and fields, but will sometimes inhabit wooded areas. They live underground in a den at the end of a burrow. Generally active in the daytime, they will dart for the safety of their burrow at any sign of danger. Two to eight young are born in the spring and when about five weeks old the appealing young-sters can be seen frolicking and closely following their parents. Groundhogs feed almost exclusively on plants. Coyotes, which also live here, find groundhogs tasty.

Insects

The large thistle patches along this section of trail are excellent places to find butterflies. A few of the butterflies you might see here are the orange sulphur, European cabbage white butterfly, painted lady, silver-spotted skipper, and one of the most spectacular, the great spangled fritillary. Although the name fritillary may be tongue-twisting, it gives an accurate description of this lovely butterfly.

Great Spangled Fritillary

Fritillary (fritl'-ary) comes from the Latin word for dice box, and spangled refers to being decorated with small, bright objects. The great spangled fritillary is one of the orange patterned butterflies; the orange wings are patterned with dice-like black dots, plus black crescents, and adorned with silver spots on the undersides.

Adult fritillaries are almost the same size as monarch butterflies, and they can be seen from June to early autumn on thistle patches, often with clouds of pastel sulphurs and skippers (both smaller butterflies, about half the size of fritillaries). Female fritillaries lay eggs on violets. The eggs hatch and develop into tiny caterpillars which overwinter and do not feed until the following spring.

Reptiles

The river and watered canal in the narrows provides suitable habitat for several species of turtles. One of the more unusual and interesting turtles to look for is the spiny softshell turtle. Unlike more familiar turtles, the spiny softshell has a roundish, pancake-like carapace (or top shell) covered by soft leathery skin rather than a horny shield. They have fully webbed, paddlelike feet. Softshells are strong swimmers and cruise the canal submerged, breathing through snouts like snorkels. Although you might be lucky to see one swimming or basking, these aggressive turtles are very fast moving and quickly escape to the water if disturbed.

Amphibians

Both the red-backed and spotted salamanders live in the narrows. Of the salamanders native to this area, the spotted is certainly one of the most striking—blue-black in color with distinct, round, yellow spots from head to tail. These salamanders are rarely seen, however, because they spend most of their lives underground. Once a year they reveal themselves during an early warm spring rain when they migrate in mass to their breeding ponds.

The red-backed salamander lives above ground and so can be seen more often, but not without some searching. In contrast to the plump spotted salamander, the red-backed is long and slender, about 2 1/2-5 inches long. Obvious from its name, it has two broad, dark-bordered red stripes from head to tail. Females lay eggs under a stone or rotten log in early summer. Eggs hatch about two months later and proceed through a larval stage to maturity in two years, omitting the aquatic stage of most amphibians.

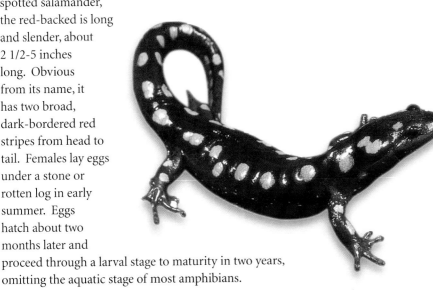

Spotted Salamander

Winter

From the beginning of fall and throughout the winter, some of the smaller woodland birds band together into small, loose foraging groups. Each species in these groups, such as black-capped chickadees, tufted titmice, white-breasted nuthatches, downy woodpeckers, brown creepers, and sometimes kinglets, travels in its own layer of forest foraging for food.

Reasons for this grouping behavior may be for informational purposes on locations of food supplies and for safety.

Black-Capped Chickadee

Lone birds in the leafless woods are more vulnerable to predators, while small flocks can be ever vigilant, sending out alarm signals when potential predators are nearby. As you move along the towpath and hear or see one of these species, look and listen for other species close by.

Topography

Geologists define river valley regions by elevation. The bottom lands include not only the river and its floodplain but adjacent flatlands not normally subject to flooding. Upland from the bottom lands are river terraces, the gently rolling terrain that is the transition between the basically level bottom lands and the steeper valley slopes. Above the slopes lies the valley top, or uplands. (See pages 40-41.)

The pinery narrows is a geological anomaly of the Cuyahoga River valley for it is only here that there are essentially no river terraces. A confined concentration of bedrock shale, highly resistant to erosion, kept the valley of the ancient Dover River steep and narrow for over two miles in length. Here, as a result, the present river valley is composed of a narrow bottom land and steep valley slopes. In many places the shale is exposed along the valley walls, particularly where eroded by the numerous small creeks and streams entering the canal from the east. The designers of State Route 82 took advantage of the narrowing of the valley when siting their graceful arched bridge. Here in the narrows the valley floor is only 400 feet wide yet at Locks 37 and 35 (north and south of the narrows) it is over 3,000 feet wide.

*There seems always to be something new to watch on the river,
something new to marvel at in the thickets and the woods.*

Helen Hayes

THE RIVER'S PLAIN

In the 2 1/2 miles between Station Road and Red Lock Trailhead we can glimpse the past in the canal remnants, overgrown roads, and stone foundations along the Ohio & Erie Canal Towpath Trail. During the canal era, 1827 to 1913, the hubbub of travelers and canawlers echoed along this active commercial route. At the southern end of this section farmers delivered loads of crops from upland fields to a canal loading dock near Red Lock.

Once the railroad was built, train whistles signaled arrival of the Valley Railroad service which dropped passengers at depots at the foot of Station Road and at Jaite on Vaughn Road. Commerce left the canal in favor of the faster and more reliable railroad, and after the canal closed for good the towpath became an access road for farmers whose fields lay along the river. Now bicycle bells and lively conversation replace the distant echoes of canawlers.

Brecksville Depot c.1923

Logging near Boston Mills. 1910.

During the canal era many of the trees were cut for fuel and building materials. Now most of the trail in this section is bordered by second and third growth forests which, in some sections, create a shaded tunnel. In contrast, just south of Lock 35 the landscape opens where the river swings away from the trail, allowing a broad sweeping view of the river valley to the west. Here a wet, shrubby meadow softens an earlier scar on the landscape. Before the National Park Service purchased this site, a topsoil removal operation used the towpath to reach its mine in the floodplain. The excavated areas close to the river were often inundated by flood waters. By the 1970s a wide wet meadow, interspersed by open ponds, lay between the towpath and the river.

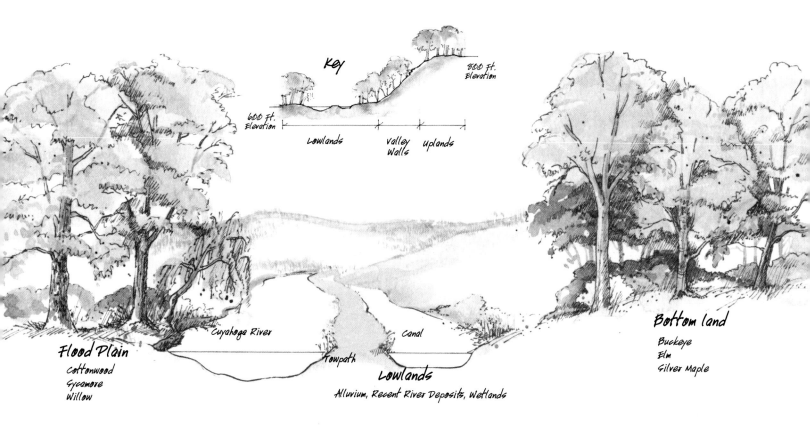

Key

800 Ft.
Elevation

600 Ft.
Elevation

Lowlands   Valley   Uplands
Walls

Flood Plain

Cottonwood
Sycamore
Willow

Cuyahoga River

Canal

Towpath

Lowlands

Alluvium, Recent River Deposits, Wetlands

Bottom land

Buckeye
Elm
Silver Maple

valley Walls
Black Walnut
Hemlock
Red Maple
Thin Soils, Exposed Bedrock

uplands
Oak, Hickory
Glacial Till Covers Bedrock

In a rather short period of time, this wet meadow has begun to support sizable shrubs and small trees. A small pond remains at the north end of the old topsoil site, somewhat hidden by the surrounding vegetation. Here great blue herons, mallards, Canada geese, and migratory waterfowl find a protected spot for feeding and resting. A bench just south of Lock 35 provides a great place for sitting and observing the activity in this changing habitat.

Throughout most of this section, floodplain forests border the trail to the west, while the slopes to the east are covered by oaks and maples favoring drier, more well-drained soils. The large cottonwoods, willows, and sycamores that are found between the trail and the river are typical of the type of trees which pioneer the "alluvial" soils found along rivers.

Cottonwoods and willows grow fast and large and have relatively soft, light wood. They help to stabilize a floodplain and after time are joined by a greater variety of hardwoods including buckeyes, elms, and maples. The type of tree in a particular area is closely related to the wetness and drainage of that spot.

Great variety in the natural world greets you along this piece of trail, from the yellow flags growing in the wetlands in spring to the stately red and white oaks branching over the canal. Snapping turtles poke their heads up out of murky canal water while eastern milk snakes daringly sun themselves on the towpath. At dusk and dawn deer venture across the trail, along with coyotes and an occasional mink or fox, all encountering a contemporary style of busyness along the historic Ohio & Erie Canal.

Birds

As is typical all along the towpath, different birds frequent different areas depending on the birds' habitat preferences. Red-winged blackbirds live in marshy areas in the floodplain. The wet meadow and pond edges at the old topsoil mine provide ideal nesting sites for these black-birds which

Red-Winged Blackbird

weave a basketlike nest just above the water, well-camouflaged in the cattails and reeds.

The males are one of the first returning migrants in early spring. They announce their territories by singing "konk-ker-ee" from the top of grass stalks and flash their red shoulder patches to attract mates. The females, easily mistaken for sparrows, are plain brown, striped birds.

It would be unusual not to see a red-tailed hawk soaring over this expanse of valley. The hawk's loud, prolonged "keeeeer" may bring your attention to the sky where the red-tailed may soar for long periods of time, wheeling higher and higher until out of sight. Recognize this large, chunky buteo by its red tail, best seen when it banks on a turn. Red-tails also can be found perched silently on dead snags surveying open ground for chipmunks, meadow voles, and white-footed mice.

The open woods both in the bottom lands and slopes are home to downy and hairy woodpeckers, two very similarly appearing black and white birds. Both are commonly seen throughout the valley and throughout the year. You are likely to hear the woodpecker hammering before you see the bird against a tree trunk or moving from tree to tree in undulating flight. The males of both species have red patches on the back of their heads; the hairy is larger than the downy and has a noticeably longer bill. All woodpeckers have very strong skulls, pointed bills, and long tongues for extracting insects and larvae from decaying wood. Much of their diet consists of plant eating insects such as wood-boring ants, beetle larvae, and small caterpillars including those of the gypsy moth.

Rose-Breasted Grosbeak

One of the most beautiful woodland birds, in song and appearance, is the male rose-breasted grosbeak. This rather solitary bird is seldom seen except in the spring when its liquid song draws attention. Roger Tory Peterson describes the lovely refrain as resembling a robin's, "but mellower, given with more feeling (as if a Robin has taken voice lessons)." The black and white pattern of feathers is accented by a rosy-red triangular breast patch, breathtaking when seen in the full light of a spring day. Like other grosbeaks, the rose-breasted has a large, thick bill designed for cracking seeds and picking off buds and caterpillars.

Flowers

Of the many plants found along the trail, three are particularly interesting and widely different: horsetail, yellow flag or iris, and Joe-pye weed. The common field horsetail is set apart from the others by its antiquity, dating back 400 million years. Much of the plant life of the Carboniferous time, when some of our coal was laid down, was of this type but much larger. The genus name, *Equisetum*, appropriately means "horse bristle," referring to the tail-like appearance of the plant stem. The 10-inch stems are noticeably jointed and rough, the roughness coming from silica taken up by the vascular stems. Horsetails grow in sterile or sandy soil and can be found year-round.

Yellow irises or flags add a sunny touch of color to the late spring landscape. These nonnative irises escaped from cultivated gardens and spread throughout the valley, forming dense stands in shallow wet places such as the abandoned canal bed or the edges of ponds north of Red Lock. They are related to a native iris, the blue flag.

In late summer, spotted Joe-pye weed lines the trail and fills wet meadows wherever it can get a foothold. Unlike the two previous plants, Joe-pye weed can grow to a height of 10 feet. It is native and has many common names stemming from its popularity among pioneers. Some sources state that it was

Field Horsetail

named after Joe Pye, a Native American living in Massachusetts in colonial times, who used the plant medicinally. It is distinctive in the summer landscape with its large clusters of smoky purplish-pink flowers atop purple spotted stems. The dried flower heads and fruits persist through the winter on the sturdy stalks.

Trees

Ohio buckeye trees can be found in many places along the entire Towpath Trail in such abundance that it's easy to overlook the fact that this species is strictly a mid-western tree. Buckeyes can be readily identified as they are the only trees along the trail with opposite compound leaves with the leaflets arranged like the spokes of a wheel. The attractive yellow blossoms in large 4 to 6-inch clusters make this tree especially easy to identify in the spring. But the most familiar characteristic of the buckeye is its fruit—the smooth "buck's eye" found hidden inside a thorny husk.

Who hasn't enjoyed picking up a buckeye and stroking its smooth dark surface, possibly pocketing it for good luck?

A small clump of young bur oaks is growing along the west side of the towpath, between Red Lock and the Old Carriage Trail intersection.

Buckeye

Bur Oak Leaf

You can also find tall, mature bur oaks growing in a row perpendicular to the entrance drive into Station Road Bridge Trailhead. Among the oaks, bur oak is relatively uncommon in the Cuyahoga valley.

45

The oak or Quercus genus of plants can be divided into two sections—white oaks and red oaks. Bur oak is one of the white oaks. White oaks differ from red oaks in that they have leaves with rounded tips (rather than the bristly tips of red oaks), hairless inner acorn shells, and acorns that mature in one year (red oak acorns take two years to mature). Most oaks can be identified by leaf shape alone, and the bur oak especially. Each leaf has one pair of deep indentations that divide the entire feather-lobed leaf into two distinct sections. The tree is also known as mossycup because of its other distinguishing feature—the acorn cup has a "bur" or "mossy" fringe of scales along the edge enclosing the acorn.

Mammals

You may often see deer here, however it is much rarer to sight a coyote. Very adaptable animals, coyotes have been reinhabiting the valley in recent years, finding adequate range

coyote

and food supplies. They are not picky eaters, including in their scavenger diet some mice, voles, rabbits, fruits, deer, garbage and carrion, such as the carcasses of road-kill deer. You are more likely to see signs of the animal rather than the coyote itself. For instance its scat, full of tricolored hair, is its calling card. Stay alert at dawn and dusk—a coyote at a distance resembles a scruffy German shepherd with drooping tail, and if you are lucky, you may hear its high-pitched yapping song or the yip-yip-yip of the youngsters.

Mink and weasels have been seen in the beaver impoundments in the valley. Minks live throughout the United States, usually in wooded areas near streams, rivers, or ponds. They are also raised in captivity for their fur and it is likely that some of the

Meadow vole

minks in the valley are descendants of minks which escaped from a mink farm. A mink has a rich brown color with a white chin patch and slightly bushy tail. It is nocturnal and a very good swimmer, feeding at night on birds, eggs, frogs, fish, and small mammals.

The least weasel is similar in appearance, with dark red-brown fur, but with all white underparts. Weasels are also active at night, but in meadows, brushy areas, and woods. They are persistent and effective mousers.

Insects

By slowing down and looking closely, you can find a number of fascinating insects along the trail. One in this area is well-known in appearance alone, another by sound, and one by its ability to "walk on water."

Perhaps the best known butterfly in this region of the state is the monarch. This reddish-brown, black, and white butterfly has gained much attention regarding its impressively long migrations. Researchers have tagged monarchs in the Cuyahoga River valley to add to the growing knowledge about their habits and travels.

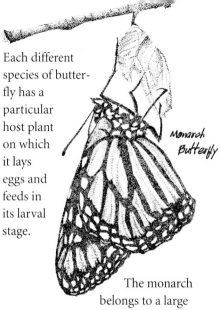

Monarch Butterfly

Each different species of butterfly has a particular host plant on which it lays eggs and feeds in its larval stage.

The monarch belongs to a large family of butterflies known as milkweed butterflies because of their host plant, milkweed—a familiar plant found in fields throughout the valley.

Milkweed butterflies are known for their strong, soaring flight, best expressed in the monarchs' migration.

Cicada Exoskeleton

The distinctive sound of summer in Ohio is the collective treetop buzzing of the annual cicadas. The nymphs of these insects live underground until they emerge as adults in July and August and make their way to nearby trees. They then climb a few feet up the trunk to molt their exoskeletons, which you may find lying on the ground. The males continue the climb to the upper branches where they take up the summer call for mates. Some periodical cicadas have a 17-year cycle, while others have a 1 to 3-year nymphal period. The 17-year cicadas collectively produce a deafening buzz when all have emerged. Their expected emergence in this part of the valley will be around 1999, not to return until 2016.

You can find water striders on just about any slow moving stream or pond in the valley. Children easily learn to recognize this long-legged insect that appears to walk on water, skirting about on the surface film in search of insects. Watching their quick erratic movements and six-dot shadows on the water's surface can be quite mesmerizing.

Water Strider

Reptiles

Turtles appeared on earth 200 million years ago, before dinosaurs. When you see a common snapping turtle at close range, it is not difficult to believe this—they have an ancient, "I've been around" look. Snappers are large turtles, up to 36 inches in length. Take their name as an appropriate warning: they have large strong heads with powerful hooked jaws that can rapidly inflict serious bites. Along with the massive head, two other characteristics can help you identify snappers—the tail is as long as the carapace and ridges of coarse scales make a saw-toothed outline along the rear of the upper shell.

Snapping Turtle

Snapping turtles bury in the mud in winter, emerging around April. In June, after mating, the females come on shore to build nests and lay eggs. During the construction of the Towpath Trail, snappers favored the freshly laid limestone trail as nest sites! You are likely to find curled eggshell remnants along the trail in spring and early summer.

Along with the snappers, several snake species are found in this area. You might see garter, water, and eastern milk snakes sunning themselves on the trail.

Amphibians

A rare and wonderful treat in nature observation is to be present when wood frogs make their annual trek to breeding ponds. On some unknown signal, very early in spring, they make their way to shallow water, and over a period of just a day or two they clamor and cluck raucously as they seek mates. Then the eggs are deposited and all is quiet again as the wood frogs return to the woods.

One of the wood frog "ponds" is the water-filled canal remnant near Goose Pond weir. At its peak, the frogs' clucking can be heard at a distance and resembles ducks quacking.

Wood Frog

Wood frogs are seldom seen other times of the year, as their tawny brown and black coloring camouflages them against the leaf litter of the forest floor.

The leopard frog is also found in ponds in the spring, but then it too heads away from the water into fields, meadows, or swampy lands. If discovered, it will flee in zigzag leaps to the safety of water. Leopard frogs are brown or green with large dark spots typically outlined in white, and two long light ridges from head to tail. They are primarily nocturnal.

Two species of salamanders are sometimes seen in this part of the valley. The two-lined salamander is found in or near creeks or seepages while the ravine salamander is completely terrestrial and lives on forested sloping hillsides—the side ravines so common in this valley.

Leopard Frog

Winter

Some birds visit the valley only in fall and winter, arriving from Canada. The dark-eyed junco (often called the snow bird) is one of these. Juncos prefer brushy areas with lots of seed. Their white tail feathers on an otherwise slate-colored body are very noticeable as they fly.

Wintertime is a good time for locating and studying galls. Galls are deformations of plants caused by insects. Insect larvae use the galls for protection and food while they are developing into adults. Many

people see galls on plants without realizing they have anything to do with insects. The formation of galls is still not thoroughly understood, but it is known that the insect through physical or chemical means somehow disrupts the growth of the plant, causing a deformation. Adult gall insects differ widely, but each species of insect causes a unique gall to form on a specific part of a particular plant species. You can tell from the appearance of the gall which insect lives within.

Three galls are very common on goldenrods: elliptical goldenrod gall, the goldenrod ball gall, and goldenrod bunch gall. The ball gall is a round swelling on the plant stem housing a grub that later develops into a small spotted-winged fruit fly. A type of moth causes the elliptical gall on the plant stem, and a midge causes the bunch gall which in the wintertime appears like a woody flower at the tip of the goldenrod stem.

The willow pine cone gall is one of the most beautiful of galls. The willow shrubs near the edge of the canal or small ponds have many of these galls which appear as tightly closed pine cones on the tips of the branches. A small midge causes this gall and overwinters in it as a larva, emerging in spring as an adult. Many other insects find galls beneficial, either preying on the insect larvae within or using the galls for shelter.

Goldenrod Galls

Elliptical

Ball

Bunch

Topography

For the most part in this section, the valley is of moderate width with a noticeable floodplain. From the west, Chippewa Creek, a major tributary of the Cuyahoga River, flows out of Brecksville Reservation and joins the river just south of Station Road Bridge. You can view the confluence of Chippewa Creek and the Cuyahoga River from the towpath, about 1/4 mile south of Station Road Bridge. Note the sand bar that has naturally formed here.

Most of the side creeks from the east flow off the steep hillside into the remains of the canal, creating a series of small ponds paralleling the trail.

Midway along the trail, Hookers Run passes under the towpath to reach the river. This fresh water cutting through a fairly mature forest attracts songbirds, mammals, and amphibians.

Chippewa Creek

Length : 8.2 Miles
Drains : 16.55 Square Miles
Average Fall : 12.3 Feet per Mile

Wallings Road
Broadway
Avery Road
I-77
SR 21
SR 82
Falls
Park Boundary
Chippewa Road Ford
Riverview Road
Valley Railway
Cuyahoga River

Each of us needs to withdraw from the cares which will not withdraw from us. We need hours of aimless wandering or spates of time sitting on park benches, observing the mysterious world of ants and the canopy of treetops.

Maya Angelou

FIELDS OF DREAMS

The 1 3/4 miles of valley between Highland Road (Vaughn Road west of the river) and Boston have seen changes in the landscape over the past three hundred years that are typical of what occurred throughout all of Ohio. The first human inhabitants in the valley, Native Americans, hunted, fished, gathered, and eventually planted small plots of corn and squash. They most likely cleared land by girdling the trees. Due to their small numbers, limited tools, and other factors, they made only minimal changes to the valley's landscape of free-flowing river and extensive forests.

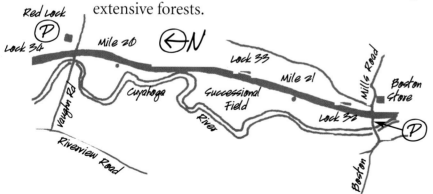

1799 marks the beginning of a dramatic change that took place in this valley and along the frontier. In that year, one of the first white settlers, David Hudson, made his way up the Cuyahoga River and disembarked near the mouth of Brandywine Creek in search of a route to his tract in the Connecticut Western Reserve. He and other early settlers were drawn to this part of the Northwest Territory by promises of cheap land with rich soil and hopes for better opportunity in this new land. They lived off the land, clearing enough of their "fields of dreams" for their own needs.

Twenty-five years later, work began on the Ohio & Erie Canal, construction that would dramatically change the valley. From the beginning of the canal era until about 1940, the area along the Ohio & Erie Canal Towpath Trail from Jaite to Boston was cleared and turned into pasture or agricultural fields. This extensive clearing resulted in spacious, open vistas.

Farming the wide open spaces. c. 1917

During this period of history, woodlands in Ohio were reduced from 24 million acres to 3.7 million acres. Wood was the basic, essential material for much of life's needs, plus much of the timber was burned in the process of clearing the forest for farms. Wood was used for homes, barns, fences, furniture, tools, barrels, and toys. With the coming of the railroad, more trees went to fuel the engines. Around 1940, this trend in reduction of the forests was reversed and forest land in Ohio has now nearly doubled over the 1940 level. As plowed and cleared lands grow into meadows and forest, the look of the land changes again here along the towpath.

This canal towpath supported mule and mule-driver traffic during the booming canal era. After the demise of the canal, this same trail was busy with farmers traveling to fields along the river and millworkers on their way to and from the Jaite paper mill near Highland Road. Even as late as the 1970s this trail that originally served the canal stayed in use as a road. Today the paper mill is silent and the fields grow wild crops.

Forests are reclaiming the river's edge and neighboring hillsides. Beavers have reinhabited the river banks and dammed sections of the canal to create new ponds. The cessation of farming and the return of the beavers have created two rich and distinct habitats along the trail: meadows and wetlands. Near Lock 33, between the trail and the river, is a particularly beautiful meadow, a land undergoing a transition. This transition is known as succession. Old field succession means that over time a plowed or mowed field will pass through predictable stages of plant and animal life, ending in the habitat's climax vegetation, in this case, hardwood forest. Given enough time, this area would return to whatever mix of trees and other plants the earliest inhabitants found, with the exception that some species have been lost to disease and others, often nonnative, have been introduced by man.

By studying the current mix of plants and animals in an old field, it is possible to deduce its history and estimate the time

Cow Parsnip   Red Tailed Hawk   White - Footed Mouse   White - Tailed Deer   Woodcock

Field Habitat

Oats   Sassafras   Turkey Vulture   Common Yellowthroat   Staghorn Sumac

of its abandonment. Many of the first plants in an abandoned field are nonnative and thrive in the unshaded sun. They are quick to cover bare ground. Some of the pioneer plants germinate best on disturbed soil and do well in poor, nutrient depleted conditions as they cannot compete well in rich soil. In each stage of succession, the mix of plants prepares the area for the next stage, and at each point along the way the plant mix meets the needs of certain animals. A killdeer may nest on the nearly bare ground the first year after an agricultural field is abandoned, while the next year field sparrows sing from an expanse of goldenrods. If the field is left unmowed, pioneer trees such as hawthorn or wild crabapple take root.

These fields have been unplowed long enough to allow black willows and other young trees to take hold. From the bench near Lock 33 you can look out over the meadow towards the Cuyahoga River. The tallest trees in the background, many of which are sycamores, outline the course of the river. In late summer and fall, goldenrod borders the trail and spreads out into the meadow. In between are grasses, cattails, sumacs, and various willows, all thriving in the open, wet meadow.

Along with the change in forest cover, drainage patterns have also been altered over the years, first by farmers and by the canal itself, and most recently by beavers damming parts of the canal and the creek flowing through the meadow. Both active and abandoned beaver lodges are found near the Jaite mill and near Locks 33 and 32. The swamp northeast of Lock 32 has been forming for nearly a century and more recently has been used by beavers and muskrats. Through their engineering, the beavers are recreating wetlands and wet meadows which benefit a variety of plants and animals.

Just south of Jaite mill is a low spot which was used as a refuse dump by the mill. When the National Park Service purchased the mill they began restoration of the area by removing the bales of discards. A small wetland formed here, fed by seepage from wells which used to serve the mill. It was the abundance of reliable well-water which prompted Charles Jaite to locate his paper mill at this location. In 1997, the National Park Service capped the water wells for safety, but you can still hear the constant, reliable flow gurgling towards the outflow pipe. The flow bypasses the former wetland which is now barely noticeable, but the tall dead trees still provide nesting holes for cavity dwelling birds.

In spring along the trail the evening air vibrates with the tinkling and ringing of tiny frog choirs while beavers tend to their construction projects. Late summer and fall finds black swallowtails drifting above the colorful mix of Queen Anne's lace, goldenrod, and sumac in the meadow, while a kestrel hovers above it all, patrolling for a meal. Near Boston, muskrats swim about the canal browsing for cattail roots or snails. From one end to the other, the trail allows you to come close to other creatures living out their lives in this landscape which has seen so many changes.

Birds

From marsh to field to tall dead trees, many different types of birds find food and nesting sites here along the trail. The return of the beaver has made a positive impact on habitat for many nesting bird species. As the beavers dam and flood sections of the canal, trees are flooded and die. Woodpeckers create cavities for nesting in these dead trees, then in subsequent years other cavity nesting birds can move into these old woodpecker homes to lay eggs and raise their own young, or just roost for the night.

Black-capped Chickadee

Among the birds that have benefited from this arrangement are woodpeckers, black-capped chickadees, tufted titmice, white-breasted nuthatches, house and Carolina

wrens, eastern bluebirds, tree swallows, great crested flycatchers, wood ducks, American kestrels, screech and barred owls, and prothonotary warblers, any of which you might see here. One of the most beautiful is the eastern bluebird, related to robins and other thrushes. The male is brilliant blue with a reddish brown breast; the female is duller and paler.

Pileated Woodpecker

You'll know the pileated woodpecker when you see him—he's the model for Woody

Woodpecker. Crow-sized, the pileated is black and white with a bright red crest. His chiseled holes tell of his presence—the pileated makes large (4 to 10 inches), rectangular or oval holes in decaying trees. Sometimes you will find large chips at the base of the tree where he has been boring for insects.

A song you might hear from the swampy thickets on either side of the trail is the "wichity, wichity" of the common yellowthroat. It is easy to hear the song, but not so easy to see this warbler. The male sports a black mask and sometimes pops up unexpectedly.

Another bird of the swampy edges is the swamp sparrow. This little sparrow, similar in

appearance to the more common song sparrow, occupies the wet meadows where it feeds on insects and seeds in the shallow water. The male generally sings from a perch atop a cattail or willow, spreading its tail as it sings.

The chimney swift's twittering sounds announce this bird over the valley. Looking like a flying cigar, the swift darts about above the wetlands catching bugs in flight. In the summer swifts seem to be in continual flight, sailing and circling, then shooting like arrows while uttering the twittering notes. Chimney swifts glue cuplike nests to the vertical insides of chimneys or hollow tree trunks. The swifts cling with sharp nails to the inside surfaces but have weak, small feet and do not perch like songbirds.

The kestrel, a type of falcon, lives along the borders of fields and woods. In the morning or late afternoon you might find him hunting over the fields. A kestrel can hover with rapidly beating wings to check out whatever is below him. When he finds suitable prey he will swoop down to grasp a mouse or insect then carry it to a perch nearby to eat.

Flowers

Queen Anne's lace is one of the most familiar plants growing in the valley. Originally a native of Asia, this plant can now be found in

Queen Anne's Lace

Europe and coast to coast in North America. Our common cultivated carrots are derived from this wild variety and the similarity can be seen in the finely divided leaves. Grown in colonial times as a vegetable,

Queen Anne's lace is now considered a weed by farmers, for its persistence edges out other planted seeds. Queen Anne's lace is the delicate white flowered companion to yellow St. Johnswort and common evening primrose in mid summer and overlaps with goldenrods that begin blooming in late summer.

Another plant familiar to early settlers is poke, known as pokeweed in the north,

Pokeweed

and poke salad in the south. Largely ignored by people today, poke used to be widely sought out and enjoyed in the spring for its tender young edible shoots. This native plant is easily recognized in late summer when it's 3 to10 feet tall and produces heads of dark purple berries. Birds feed on the berries, but please beware: they are **poisonous** to humans.

Sensitive ferns can be found in many places throughout the valley. The sensitive fern has been described as an unfernlike fern, having rather sturdy, coarse leaves. It likes damp or wet places, in full sun or shade, and can be very abundant in meadows and along muddy seeps.

Sensitive Ferns

Trees

In this section of the trail you will find trees that are common along the entire length of Towpath Trail—sycamores, willows, Ohio buckeyes, box elders, and staghorn sumacs.
  Some are significant not because of their particular beauty or attributes, but because in death they continue to contribute to the overall ecology of the place. The dead snags which are still standing in the wet areas provide shelter for squirrels, raccoons, bats, and many different birds. Fallen, rotting logs house small animals, ants, termites, and other insects. Mosses, lichens, and mushrooms live off the log and in turn help to decompose it, changing tree trunk into soil.

Mammals

Beaver, muskrats, and an occasional mink can all be found in this area, making use of the water confined in the canal basin. The beaver and muskrat can be easily confused when seen in the water, however, the beaver is a much larger, heavier mammal with a broad, thick paddlelike tail compared to the smaller muskrat with a narrow, compressed tail. You might see muskrats during the day, while beavers usually emerge from their lodges at dusk and work until dawn.

Insects

Black Swallowtail

Tiger Swallowtail

Abundant Queen Anne's lace along the trail makes certain that you have a good chance of seeing one of the largest, most striking butterflies in this region, the black swallowtail. This butterfly's black wings are lined with a double row of yellow spots. You can find black swallowtails floating low over the meadows. Plants in the carrot family host this species of butterfly.

A close relative, the tiger swallowtail has a reverse patterning of yellow wings with black tigerlike stripes. The plump, green caterpillar of this butterfly spins a mat on a tree leaf then wraps it about him for shelter. Two of

its favorite host trees are willow and cottonwood, both abundant along this section of trail.

Mantids are large predaceous insects, mostly found in the tropics. The praying mantis found here in the north is an introduced species, native to Europe. The mantis' forelegs, held as if in prayer, are used to hold prey, while the hind legs are used for walking and leaping. An interesting find in the wild are the mantis' egg cases, straw colored papier-mache like masses attached to weeds or boards. The eggs overwinter, hatch in the spring, and hundreds of little mantids emerge, many of them soon to be eaten by their siblings. Look for mantids on the foliage and flowers of meadow plants.

The energetic whirligig beetle inhabits watered sections of canal. While the praying mantis is almost nonchalant in its slow movements, the

Praying Mantis

whirligig beetle is "wired." These beetles have short paddlelike hind legs that whirl them about erratically on the surface of the water. The beetles often cluster together, swimming in circles, noticeable even from a distance due to the sparkling, dappled effect they make on the water's surface.

The red-legged grasshopper is found in meadows and open pastures. It is appropriately named, with bright red coloring along its lower hind legs. The upper hind legs have a herringbone pattern.

Eastern Painted Turtle

Reptiles

Painted turtles, common all along the trail, prefer to live in slow-moving waters with soft bottoms and submerged logs—a perfect description of the canal. Painted turtles are the ones you are most likely to see lined up on logs, sunning themselves. Their carapaces are oval and smooth, olive to black in color, and bordered with olive, yellow, or red markings. They have yellow and red stripes on their necks, legs, and tails. To tell the difference between an eastern painted turtle and the closely related midland painted turtle, look at the patterning of the scutes—the plates of the turtle's shell. Eastern's scutes are arranged in straight rows, while the midland's are arranged alternating like bricks.

Amphibians

Through early spring to early summer, three amphibians take their turns filling the night air with music as they call for mates. The tiny

Chorus Frog

spring peeper, about one inch long, is very difficult to observe, however, when a chorus gathers in early spring the combined voices can be heard a quarter mile away. An individual call is a high-pitched whistle, while together the spring peepers sound like jingling bells. The males usually call from shrubs or small trees near the edges of marshes and shallow ponds.

The time of the year when the spring peepers sing closely corresponds to blooming of the pussy willow. When the pussy willows are gray and just starting to bloom, the peepers sing; when a scattering of seeds appears on the willows in mid-May, the peepers stop singing.

Chorus frogs, also very tiny, often accompany the spring peepers. The chorus frog's call has been best described as the sound of a fingernail running up the teeth of a comb. Both species dart for safety at the slightest noise, and only by patiently watching and waiting at the edge of their ponds can you make their acquaintance.

The common gray tree frog is heard a little later in the season, and its call too is unmistakable once you learn it—a hearty, melodious trill. Tree frogs, as their name indicates, live high in trees, descending only at night to call and breed. This frog's scientific name, *Hyla versicolor,* refers to the fact that the gray tree frog can change its color from gray to brown to green.

Winter

Sensitive fern produces a very hardy spore-bearing stalk which persists throughout winter. This fern gained its name because the sterile leaves die off at the first frost, leaving only the

Sensitive Ferns in Winter

erect, beadlike, fertile spikes standing. The spore-bearing stalk does not resemble the summer fronds at all—it looks like a stick with branchlets of brown capsules containing thousands of spores.

The familiar Queen Anne's lace flower heads open and close in relation to the surrounding moisture in the air. In winter you can look for the flower heads which have closed for the last time. The bracts close around the seeds in what is known as a "bird's nest." The seeds have rows of spines which facilitate their dispersal, as they catch onto the fur of animals passing by.

Both meadow voles and short-tailed shrews are common in the valley, but the only time you are likely to see signs of them is during the winter months. Shrews are the smallest and most common mammal in North America. They need to hunt nearly continuously to keep up their body warmth. In winter, when there is snow on the ground, both shrews and voles make snow tunnels for warmth and protection from predators. As the top layer of snow melts, you can see these tunnels marking the animals' travels. When the snow thaws you might even find the voles' winter nest. In warm months, voles move underground to nest, but still construct runways beneath the meadow grasses to provide access to their diet of grass.

Shrews, voles, and white-footed mice will also leave their tiny footprints on the snow's surface. Both the mice and shrews sometimes drag their tails, leaving a delicate stitching pattern in the snow.

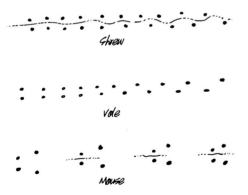

Shrew

Vole

Mouse

Topography

Brandywine Creek, one of the valley's major tributaries, enters from the east, flowing under the trail just 100 yards or so south of Highland Road (look for a break in the tree line east of the trail).

Length : 11.5 Miles
Drains : 26.21 Square Miles
Average Fall : 35.6 Feet per Mile

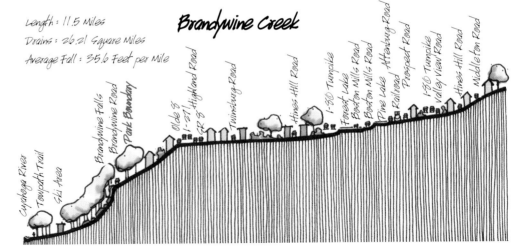

Brandywine Creek

Cuyahoga River
Towpath Trail
Ski Area
Brandywine Falls
Brandywine Road
Park Boundary
Olde 8
I-271
CR 5 Highland Road
Twinsburg Road
Hines Hill Road
I-80 Turnpike
Forest Lake
Boston Mills Road
Boston Mills Road
Pine Lake
Attenburg Road
Railroad
Prospect Road
I-80 Turnpike
Valley View Road
Hines Hill Road
Middleton Road

69

Brandywine Creek Aqueduct

This run drains over 26 square miles and is the third largest of all tributaries of the Cuyahoga River (the Little Cuyahoga and Tinkers Creek are first and second). Some say the creek's name, given by early settlers, reflected the dark brandy color of the water which was the result of tannin leaching from the many hemlocks in the area. Others say it came from the fact that a distillery was once located on the banks of the falls, Brandywine being another name for whiskey.

Take the opportunity to see the craftsmanship in the stonework of the Brandywine Aqueduct. This stone arched culvert is best observed by moving off the trail to the east, looking back to where the creek slips under the towpath.

*To be a good naturalist one must be a stroller
or a creeper, or better still a squatter in every
sense of the word.*

Charles William Beebe

LIFE IN THE SLOW LANE

During the height of the canal era, two active canal villages anchored the ends of this section of the towpath as they do today: Boston at the north end and Peninsula at the south. Sounds of sawing and hammering issued from the boatyards, heard above the voices of men unloading packet boats. By the middle of the twentieth century the heavy sounds of construction equipment replaced these now silenced voices, as the immense twin bridges of I-271 and the Ohio Turnpike were erected high over the Cuyahoga valley.

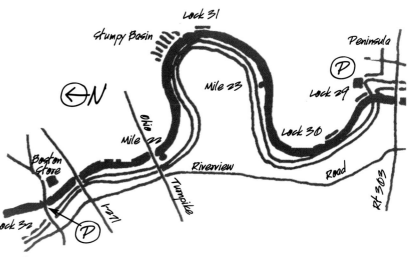

The excavation for the highways cleared and altered the northern part of this section, while the southern half remained wilder and forested.

Large amounts of topsoil were removed during construction of the highways, leaving very sterile ground remaining. Since the establishment of Cuyahoga Valley National Recreation Area, the National Park Service has completed erosion control restoration projects beneath the bridges. Now these once scarred areas are spacious grasslands bordering the trail. It is interesting to see that because of the sterility of the soil, the process of succession is slowed, and after 20 years there is still only grass where in a more fertile soil you would find shrubs and small trees.

Boston, Ohio C. 1910

Peninsula, Ohio c. 1901

Underneath and south of the highway bridges the canal still holds water. Here in "turtle alley" you can often find numerous turtles sunning themselves, spring through fall. Towards Peninsula, the Ohio & Erie Canal Towpath Trail, via a boardwalk, enters a unique area long known as Stumpy Basin. The basin was a wide place in the canal, a turning basin used for boats to pass or turn. It is believed that due to all the boat activity a mix of seeds were dispersed here over time, resulting in an interesting flora in and near the remaining wetland and the nearby wooded slopes. The heavily wooded area between the basin and Peninsula is especially beautiful in the early spring when ephemerals, the delicate early wildflowers, line the edges of the canal bed and towpath.

Turtle Alley

In three places, just south of Boston, at Stumpy Basin, and farther south near Lock 30, the original towpath is nonexistent or obscured. The Cuyahoga River, in its natural meandering, has over time cut through the narrow band of land that separated the canal from the river. In all three places the trail has been rerouted and reconstructed. In Stumpy Basin you can see the broken ends of the former towpath at either end of the new boardwalk, a dramatic illustration of how much the river has moved over the years. Similarly, north of Lock 30 where the path is edged with a wooden railing, you can observe where the old towpath disappears. In this case the river cut through the bank and back again, leaving an island with the old towpath obscured in the vegetation. A channel of the river now flows through what used to be the canal, next to the new path. Both areas continue to change, especially Stumpy Basin where the river continues to work into the basin, and the basin itself is filling with soil and plants.

From one end of trail to the other, there is great contrast, from the soothing sound of the shaded river riffles to the buzz of grasshoppers in the exposed open fields, from the delicate tiny blossoms of spring ephemerals to the towering Joe-pye weeds and great angelicas, and from the distantly glimpsed shale cliffs along the river to the immediacy of the mud bottom of Stumpy Basin. Look high and low for the multitude of nature that surrounds you as you explore the next 2 1/2 miles.

Lock 31

Towpath

Turning Basin

Stumpy Basin—1851

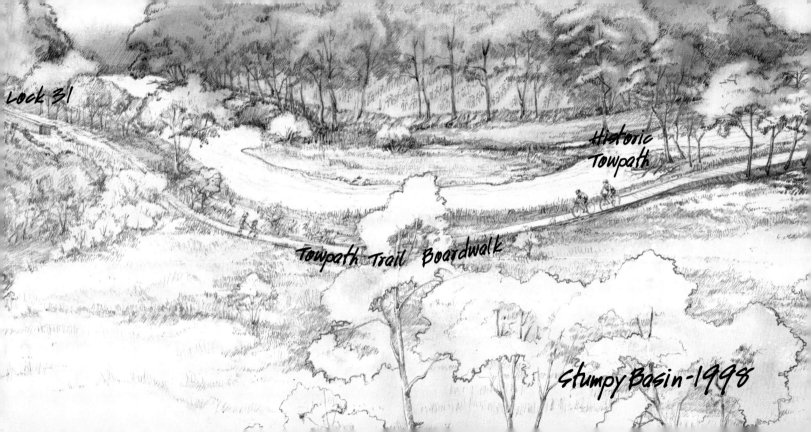

Lock 31

Historic
Towpath

Towpath Trail Boardwalk

Stumpy Basin - 1998

Birds

The variety of open fields, shrubby areas, swamp, river edge, and tall trees welcomes an equally diverse company of birds to this area. One of these, the brown-headed cowbird, is from one of a few families of birds which do not build their own nests but use other birds' nests, a behavior called brood parasitism. The cowbird, called lazy-bird in some parts of the country, lays its eggs in the nest of another bird when the nest is unguarded. Sometimes it pushes out the host's eggs. Usually the host bird raises the cowbird young along with her own. Since the young cowbird is often larger and more vigorous than the host bird's chicks, it more successfully competes for nourishment from the parent bird.

Yellow Warbler

One of the hosts to the cowbirds is the yellow warbler, a flashy little warbler which nests in the shrubs and saplings throughout the valley. Although cowbirds attempt to use the yellow warblers' nests, the warblers often outsmart the cowbirds. Apparently recognizing the foreign egg, the warbler will build a new floor to its nest and lay a new brood. These warblers help control populations of many of the caterpillars which are destructive to plants, such as cankerworms and other "measuring worms." Yellow warblers appear all yellow from a distance, but on close inspection the males have very pretty chestnut streaks on their breasts and sides.

Of the woodpeckers commonly found along the trail, the northern flicker is a little unusual, for you are just as likely to see it on the ground as clasping a tree trunk. Flickers eat more ants than any other bird, and you can often see them hopping about on the ground in fields or open woods, probing for ants. When it flies up from the ground, the flicker flashes a white rump patch. The flicker is mostly brown, unlike our other black and white woodpeckers, and it has a conspicuous black crescent across the breast.

Finally, you might catch sight of some swallows in this section of trail.

Twittering swallows sweep low over the river hawking insects. Their long, powerful wings and small feet reflect the fact that they spend most of their waking hours in the air. Most of the names of the various swallows indicate where they live— you can see barn, bank, tree, and northern rough-winged swallows along the river during the summer. In September they leave to spend the winter in South America.

Flowers

Of all the places along the towpath, the area between Stumpy Basin and Lock 30 is particularly favored in the springtime for the display of delicate wildflowers lining the trail. These early wildflowers are known as ephemerals, due to their brief appearance. They are also natives to the region, allowing you to view plant combinations similar to those seen by the earliest inhabitants of the valley. It is a pleasant challenge to see how many different wildflowers you can find along the trail in early spring.

One of the tiniest of these early flowers is the spring beauty. You have to be on the lookout to spot these delicate plants. The flowers are just 1/2 inch across and have white petals with pink lines. In early spring, they carpet the edges of the path.

Squirrel corn, emerging about the same time, has a very different appearance. White, kernel-shaped flowers dangle from stems amid finely divided parsley-like leaves. Squirrel corn is related to the cultivated plant called bleeding heart.

Squirrel Corn

Large-flowered trillium appears in early May. The trillium name refers to the whorl of three large leaves, three large showy white petals, and three green sepals. Trilliums grow in rich woods, especially favoring the forested slopes such as those on the far side of the canal. It is believed that

Shortly after Europeans began exploring and colonizing North America, the plant life of the two continents began to mix. Colonists sent American species back home to Europe for study and reproduction, and in turn brought to North America seeds of their favorite plants. Other seeds came accidentally, attached to clothing or animals or in imported grains and goods. Over the early centuries of settlement, these new plants moved westward along with the pioneers.

Today, of all the plants growing in Cuyahoga Valley National Recreation Area, about 22% are alien, or nonnative. Several nonnative species, if left unchecked, could pose a major threat to native species. These are known as "invasives," implying that they have the potential for taking over an area, crowding out native species. This can throw an ecosystem out of balance, as the newcomer spreads rapidly and upsets the mix of plants and animals which have evolved over time.

You can find four of these invasive nonnative plants along the Towpath Trail. These plants are being monitored by National Park Service resource management specialists. In some cases, attempts are being made to eradicate or at least control the invasive plants. All these plants are difficult to remove successfully by manual means, such as cutting them or digging them up. Dealing with aliens is one place where land managers resort to the selective use of specific herbicides.

European alder buckthorn, *Rhamnus frangula*, is another native of Europe which has escaped from cultivation and tends to take over.

It is a deciduous shrub, growing to about 20 feet.

Purple loosestrife, *Lythrum salicaria*, in itself is quite attractive, however it has the ability to spread rapidly and completely take over a wetland, turning a diverse plant system into a monoculture. It grows 3 to 6 feet and has showy, magenta flower spikes. It is a native of Europe.

Japanese knotweed, *Polygonum cuspidatum*, is a native of Japan which was planted in North America as an ornamental and now has spread rapidly. You will find it in very extensive stands along the banks of the river. In the spring, the flower clusters on this tall perennial cast a pretty haze along the river, and in the fall they cover the banks with a rusty shade, but like other nonnatives, the knotweed is taking over where native plants once grew.

Giant reed grass or *Phragmites australis* is native to North America, but not to this region. It is usually found in salt marshes or in brackish water. It is easy to identify as it is the tallest grass you will find in wet areas along the trail. It grows up to 13 feet and has stiff leaves on coarse, hollow stems. It is topped by a plumelike flower cluster. The use of road salt has made many inland wetlands alkaline enough for this grass to flourish. It tends to push out cattails which are an important food source for native animals.

81

large-flowered trilliums are declining in the valley due to the overabundance of deer which feed on the plants.

The Jack-in-the-pulpit is an easy flower to recognize because of its distinctive appearance, having a green and purple hood curving over a club-shaped spadix, resembling a "Jack" in a pulpit. Later in the summer only the fruit remains—a bright cluster of red berries atop a stiff, green stalk.

Jack-in-the-Pulpit

-Fall-

-Spring-

In early spring search the layer of dried leaves on the ground alongside the trail to find the first sprouts of Mayapples. The tightly wound leaf clusters emerge through last year's leaf litter, sometimes carrying a poked leaf right up off the ground. Around mid-May the umbrella-like leaves unfurl, hiding the single white flower. The leaves can be up to a foot wide, growing from stalks up to 1 1/2 feet tall.

Dame's Rocket

Later in spring and early summer, two other plants can be found in this part of the valley: dame's rocket and wild blue phlox. Dame's rocket, not a native flower, escaped from early gardens and now carpets

large areas of the valley along the river. It is very showy, 2 to 3-feet high, with white to purple flowers, each flower with four petals. The toothed leaves are alternate on the stalk.

Dame's Rocket

Several species of phlox are native to this area, but are also cultivated in gardens At first glance, some people mistake dame's rocket for garden phlox, but garden phlox blooms later than dame's rocket, its leaves are entire (not toothed) and are opposite on the stalk. Garden phlox has magenta-pink flowers, each with five petals. Another phlox found in the valley, wild blue phlox, blooms earlier than the

82

garden phlox. Wild blue phlox grows to about 1 1/2 feet tall and like garden phlox, blue phlox flowers have five petals, the leaves are entire, and they are opposite on the stalk.

Wild Blue Phlox

Mammals

Most of the mammals common to the valley can be found here along the trail. Both beavers and muskrats inhabit the canal prism where it still holds water. Signs of beaver activity have also been seen on the island visible from the trail north of Lock 29. Deer and raccoon are also common. Raccoons den in hollow trees and prefer to live in woods near streams. You might find their hand-like footprints in the soft mud along the river banks where they hunt for crayfish and other aquatic animals. The dried and curled remains of turtle eggs can also be a sign of raccoons having raided a nest for a meal.

Mussel Shell

Coon Tracks

Insects

Insects or their signs can be observed throughout the year. One of the delights of an early spring walk is finding the very first butterfly. The earliest butterfly in this area is the mourning cloak, a pretty butterfly with brown to purple wings edged in yellow. Watch for the mourning cloak on an early spring day, whenever the temperature

Mourning Cloak

rises above 60°F. These butterflies, unlike most others, overwinter in the shelter of loose bark or a rock crevice in deciduous woods. In the first warmth of spring they emerge and flutter about, seeking nutrition from tree sap or early flowers.

Another early spring insect you can observe in woodland areas is the bumblebee, and for similar reasons. The fertilized queen bumblebee also overwinters and emerges on the first warm days of spring. She then proceeds to fly in a meandering pattern, buzzing loudly, looking for flower nectar and a suitable nest site. With careful observation and luck, you might locate the nest by following the queen. She will form a nest of grasses, mosses, and leaves in an old burrow such as a chipmunk hole. She then collects pollen, lays the eggs on the pollen, covers them with wax and sits on them, warming them until the baby bees hatch several days later.

The bee fly is not a bee but a fly! With its stout, furry body it resembles a small bumblebee, but is all velvety black. Bee flies can be found in meadows or fields, feeding on flower nectar or resting on the ground.

In summer, the black-horned tree cricket joins the chorus of other crickets which fill the night air. You are not likely to see this cricket, but can enjoy its loud summer singing. In the winter, look for the egg-laying sites— these appear like little zipper openings on pencil-width twigs of berry bushes or other field shrubs and trees. Fresh egg sites will be on live twigs while old sites will be empty and the twig above the site may be weathered and dead.

The fall webworm, one of the tiger moths, is one insect that you are most likely to get to know in its larval form rather than adult form. The larvae spin a communal nest

Fall Webworm

Tent Caterpillars

84

of silk over the end of a leafy tree branch, then remain inside and feed on the leaves until ready to emerge and individually pupate. The silky nests resemble those of the eastern tent caterpillar, however the tent caterpillars spin their nests in the fork of a tree and leave the nest to feed.

Reptiles

Along with the commonly found painted turtles and snapping turtles, you may occasionally find a terrestrial turtle, the eastern box turtle. Box turtles live in moist woodlands and can also be found in floodplains of side streams or the river. The best chance of seeing a box turtle is early in the morning

Eastern Box Turtle

or after a rain. They can be easily overlooked in the woods, camouflaged by their mottled tan, brown, and orange coloring against dried leaf litter. Listen for their slow rustling through the dry leaves during summer. If conditions are favorable, a box turtle can live to a ripe old age of 50.

Amphibians

American toads can be found in this and other parts of the valley, especially in spring when they seek out watered places to breed and lay eggs. Though fairly secretive the rest of the year, in springtime the male toads reveal themselves by trilling beautifully and persistently to attract females. Toads eat primarily insects and therefore have earned a reputation as the best residents of a garden. The tiny 2/5 inch newly metamorphosed toads leave the breeding ponds in early summer and disperse throughout the woodlands.

Unlike the toads, green frogs will always be found in or near water. They mate more quietly than the toads; females lay eggs in pond areas such as the canal and pond just north of Stumpy Basin.

Spring peepers also come to the water to call for mates in the early, still chilly spring evenings. The scientific name for this tiny tree frog is *Pseudacris crucifer crucifer*, referring to the dark cross pattern on its back. Spring peepers hibernate during the winter, secure under logs and leaf litter.

Winter

From historic accounts and photos we learn that the slow-moving canal water froze in the winter, providing ice for refrigeration and ice-skating for recreation. In addition to forming ice, winter's cold also transforms moisture into frost and snow. Actually, you can observe snow year-round by looking up at the sky! Cirrus clouds are made of ice crystals and the upper portions of heavy rain clouds often consist of snow or hail.

Two types of frost are particularly interesting to observe. When moisture oozes from the ground and the air temperature is very cold, the moisture freezes into masses of columnar frost resembling thick locks of white hair emerging from the ground. You are most likely to see this in the early spring when the temperature drops below freezing following a thaw.

Hoarfrost is the name given the delicate, fernlike ice crystals which grow on plant stems, branches, and other surfaces when moist air encounters very cold air. For instance, on an early winter morning near the Cuyahoga River, river mist rises, encounters the colder air above the river, and crystallizes along the tree limbs closest to the river, decorating the branches with ephemeral white lace.

Ten categories of snow are listed in the International Snow Classification. The most familiar of these—and the most aesthetically pleasing—are called "plates" and "stellars," the cut paper snowflakes from grade school days. Skiers have their own names for different types of snow. Snow which falls then

What is in a Snowflake?

Snowflakes are composed of individual snow crystals which can, depending on their shape and moisture content, remain as individual crystals or interlock into larger snowflakes, some as large as two inches in diameter. The basic building block of a snow crystal, the ice crystal, is actually transparent. Snow appears white because the many surfaces of the crystals reflect light.

Snow crystals can form in clouds when temperatures are anywhere between 32° and -39°F. The final crystal shape

depends on the temperature and humidity of the air where the crystal is formed. For example, cold air with little moisture is the perfect condition for the formation of small column crystals; warmer air with lots of moisture will more likely form the larger stellar crystals. It is common for a crystal to pass through different atmospheric conditions before reaching the ground; this will lead to the formation of combination crystals. Here are illustrated five simple crystals and three combination crystals. Note the predominance of six-sided shapes in the makeup of the crystals: this comes from the basic crystalline form of water, a hexagon.

Crystals are best observed by catching snowflakes on a cool, dark surface, like the arm of your insulated jacket. A small hand lens can help you see some of the details and smaller crystals, but avoid getting too close—you may melt them with your breath!

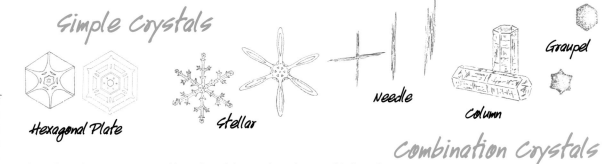

Simple Crystals

Hexagonal Plate

Stellar

Needle

Column

Graupel

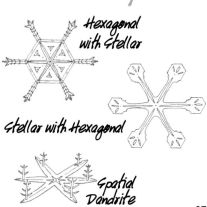

Combination Crystals

Hexagonal with Stellar

Stellar with Hexagonal

Spatial Dandrite

melts and recrystallizes is called "corn snow." "Powder" refers to the fresh, dry snow of lowest density which is formed when large and perfectly symmetrical stellar crystals fall in calm air in single-digit temperatures.

Hoarfrost on The Cuyahoga

Topography

Along this section of trail, the directional trend of the Cuyahoga River continues to be north and south, but a particularly sweeping meander of the river causes the trail to trend east and west. This meander carves a large "S" into the landscape, placing Stumpy Basin due north of the river though it may feel as if you are still east of the river.

In several places the river is in contact with bedrock, Mississippian shale. This shale was once the silty bed of an ancient river, the Dover River, which predates the glacial ice ages and the post-glacial Cuyahoga River. The best place to view the meeting of the ancient and "modern" river channels is from the trail bridge over the Cuyahoga River at Lock 29 in Peninsula. Here you can see how the Cuyahoga is cutting downward and outward through the Mississippian shale bedrocks which held the ancient Dover River. The shale you see today would have been exposed at the western side of the Dover River valley; the bedrock on the eastern side is covered with deposits from an ancient glacial lake. Today's Cuyahoga River is now cutting its own valley into this ancient landscape.

To the attentive eye, each moment of the year has its own beauty, and in the same field, it beholds, every hour, a picture which was never seen before, and which shall never be seen again.

Ralph Waldo Emerson

WHERE CORN IS KING

You cannot walk or ride the 3 miles from Peninsula to Everett without being reminded of one of the primary attractions this valley presented to settlers migrating from the east in the early 1800s. The reports of rich, flat bottom lands, prime for agriculture, appealed strongly to eastern farmers struggling with depleted, rocky soils. Letters from early settlers and boosters stressed Ohio's mild climate, rich soil, huge trees, and equally huge crop yields. The land was also cheap.

Searching for better opportunities, New Englanders purchased their lands sight unseen, made the arduous journey, and began new lives in the Ohio wilderness. The first tasks upon arriving were to clear land, erect a cabin, and plant wheat.

But even long before these settlers arrived in the valley, Native Americans in small, permanent settlements were planting and harvesting corn, beans, and pumpkins. Today, hundreds of years later, the Szalay family continues to offer these same crops to customers who make their annual pilgrimages to the farm stand in the little hamlet of Everett.

One of the first permanent settlers in this part of the valley was Jonathan Hale. Hale emigrated from Connecticut to the Western Reserve in 1810 and to historians' good fortune his diaries, account books, and some correspondence were preserved by his descendants. His homestead, now an historic site operated by the Western Reserve Historical Society, is located less than two miles from Everett and the Hunt Farm Visitor Information Center. Riverview Road, which parallels the Towpath Trail from Peninsula to Hunt Farm, closely follows the route of one of the earliest roads along the river, a road which Hale proposed, linking Boston to the Cuyahoga Portage in present day Merriman Valley.

During Hale's lifetime, the construction of the Ohio & Erie Canal altered the landscape in ways that remain evident today. Besides adding the "big ditch," the canal construction also precipitated a change in the vegetation mix of the Everett area, from mostly native forest to the current combination of second or third growth forest, agricultural fields, and escaped domestic plants. Agriculture dominated this area from around 1850 to 1930, during which time the major crops were wheat, oats, and corn. The wheat was for human consumption in the form of flour, while the oats fed the horses, and the corn fed pigs and cows. The corridor you travel today is the same one that those commodities traveled 150 years ago, the oats and wheat on their way to Peninsula to be ground into meal, the flour and other products on their way to

markets as far away as New York City. The canal carried waves of new settlers into the interior, raised the value of the settlers' surplus crops, and made it possible for them to purchase fabrics, furniture, and farm equipment from eastern factories.

Today along the trail connecting the village of Peninsula and the crossroads hamlet of Everett, the mixture of

planted fields, woodland, and swampy canal prism provides habitat for numerous animals, from deer and coyotes to crows and phoebes. For most of the distance, the landscape is broad and flat to the east, while to the west the hills rise sharply to Oak Hill. The sounds of the river's rapids accompany you at the north end, while Furnace Run's more placid riffles greet you to the south.

In between, crows fly up from the cultivated fields in raucous confusion at the crack of the corn cannons while you travel along, well shaded by cottonwoods and willows. Many different vines which disappear from view in the summertime, intertwined in the mass of growing plants, come out into view in fall and winter, now distinct from their neighbors and offering much needed nutrition to overwintering birds. Go slow here for the details that would be lost in a hurried visit.

Birds

It is a rare day that you do not see or hear an American crow in the vicinity of Hunt Farm. One of the most adaptable of all birds, this fearless black bird frequents corn fields throughout the park. Crows are often seen along the road as well, feeding on traffic-killed animals. In the fall you can hear them noisily congregating in large roosts. Besides their familiar "caw," they also mimic other sounds such as the human voice or whine of a dog.

The most predominant bird along the trail is the song sparrow. It is a perky bird with a striped breast and characteristic black "stick-pin." Look for it flitting about in swampy, brushy areas of the canal prism. It often sings its lovely song from a perch atop a bush. Song sparrows return to the valley from their southern wintering grounds earlier than most other birds, often by

Song Sparrow

late February, and some remain year-round. The eastern phoebe is also fairly easy to find and identify, being very predictable in its nesting. Phoebes are among the first returning spring migrants that you will hear—listen for a phoebe to call out its name, in a raspy, low two-noted "fee-bee." This plain looking bird often nests under bridges and will return to the same spot year after year. A phoebe will characteristically pump its tail as it perches, waiting to snap up flying insects.

The Deep Lock Quarry area is known for its warblers—tiny, small, insect-eating birds. One of the earliest and easiest warblers to find there and all along the trail is the yellow-rumped warbler. Yellow-rumps eat insects and berries,

and particularly favor poison ivy berries! These whitish berries are easy to see in the fall, drooping from the twining vines, and they are one reason that the yellow-rumped warblers hang around the valley the longest before migrating south.

Quite in contrast to the yellow-rumped warbler, the hooded warbler which also nests in Deep Lock Quarry is a much more secretive bird.

Hooded Warbler

You are more likely to hear its lovely, clear "weeta weeteo" song than to see this bird. Its name comes from the appearance of the male: all yellow with a deep black "hood" about its face.

Two other birds found along the trail are forest inhabitants, also more often heard than seen. Their songs alone evoke the sights and sounds and smells of a woods in the warm days of summer. The eastern wood pewee repeats its name in a plaintive, rising and falling "pee-ah-wee, pee-urrr," while the red-eyed vireo talks incessantly in short little phrases, "here I am, look at me, you see it?..." In midday, in the hottest days of summer, when all else is silent, this vireo repeats its phrases.

Flowers

Flowering plants can be found along the trail from early spring right up to the first hard frost. One of the very earliest is coltsfoot, a plant with dandelionlike yellow flowers which appear before the leaves. Coltsfoot grows on the berms of the towpath and on other bare, sunny banks.

coltsfoot

Forget-me-nots have tiny blue flowers with yellow eyes. Some may have escaped from gardens and do well in the swampy parts of the canal. They bloom from late spring to fall,

Forget-me-nots

adding a delicate spot of color to the blanket of green in the canal bed.

Asters signal autumn, and two species in particular grow in abundance along the trail: New York and New England asters. Of the many different species of asters, the New England aster is one of the most stunning; its deep purple flowers with yellow centers are carried atop a stout, hairy stem, 2 to 7 feet high. The New York aster is also quite beautiful, with dark blue flowers on a smooth, slender stem, shorter than the New England aster. The white asters, also called frost asters, survive the frosts and are the last flowers to bloom before winter.

Vine aficionados will find this section of Towpath Trail especially appealing: at least ten different species of vines can be found twining and twisting, all easily seen from the path,

New England Asters

some most visible in summer but others better seen in fall or winter when their dried forms distinguish them from nearby plants. For obvious reasons, one of the most important vines to recognize is poison ivy. This vigorous vine's rootlets attach themselves to trees and other vertical supports. One of poison ivy's identifying characteristics any time of year is the twining vine itself, noticeably hairy and sometimes as thick as 4 inches. Some truly outstanding specimens can be found just adjacent to the trail. The plant's oil is responsible for the nasty contact poisoning that afflicts many who have brush-ins with poison ivy. Unlike humans, birds are not adversely affected by the poison and many species feed on the white berries which persist through winter.

Another common vine frequently found with poison ivy is Virginia creeper. While poison ivy has three leaflets, Virginia creeper has five. It climbs to great heights in trees by attaching its disk tendrils to the tree bark. Both Virginia creeper and poison ivy are spectacular in the fall when they turn bright red, preceding other fall color.

The rich red vines outline the still-green support trees.

Virgin's bower is the poetic name given to wild clematis. It tends to trail over adjoining shrubs and is most noticeable in the fall when the female flowers develop feathery tails that curve into airy, loose balls. Because of this, Virgin's bower is also known as devil's hair and old-man's-beard.

Virgin's Bower

Trees

White pines are not usually found along river banks, but just north of Deep Lock you can find an unexpected grove of white pines, probably planted by a former resident. The warm, pungent scent of the fallen pine needles may draw you off the towpath and into the filtered light beneath these evergreens. Many people associate the sighing of wind with the pines, and in many ways this is appropriate, for in any season the needle-laden branches give voice to the breeze, and the cones of the white pine rely on the wind for pollination. Sometimes in April or May you can even see the faint clouds of golden pollen drifting about the trees.

While white pines are usually hillside trees, cottonwoods love the mucky lowlands and are not harmed by periodic flooding and silting. They, along with their relatives the willows, help to reforest and stabilize river banks and new islands.

Cottonwoods also depend on the wind, in this case to disperse their downy seeds.

Eastern Cottonwood

Sugar Maples

Once you've experienced the rain of early summer "cotton," you'll not forget it. Young cottonwoods can grow as much as five feet in one year and attain large diameters, but are not particularly long-lived.

Sugar maples grow along the west side of the towpath, just north of Deep Lock. They distinguish themselves from surrounding trees in autumn when they reveal their brilliant yellow, orange, and red leaf colors. The various colors are dependent on available light: redder hues appear in the sunniest parts of the trees while shaded areas yield the oranges and yellows.

Mammals

Where corn is king, deer are loyal subjects, much to the chagrin of farmers. Deer are vegetable eaters and find the sweet corn as delectable as do the hundreds of customers at the corn stand. Watch for deer at dusk—when alarmed they will raise their white tails, flashing the "flag," and can race off as fast as 35 to 40 miles per hour.

Coyotes have returned to the Cuyahoga River valley in recent years. They are highly adaptive predators and scavengers, eating a wide variety of foods including mice, rabbits, fruits, very young deer, road-killed deer, and garbage.

Ruthless hunting of coyotes has not daunted them—their present range in North America is more widespread than it was before the arrival of the Mayflower. They have even adapted to living near cities.

Red Fox

The habitat along the towpath is ideal for them—open fields to hunt in and nearby woods for cover and denning.

Although there are over 60 coyotes in the park (and with increasing numbers) you are more likely to find signs of them, such as their scat, than to see them. If you are out at night you might be treated to their song—a wild, high pitched call that may begin with a few barks and be accompanied by pups in a staccato yapping.

This farm field/woods habitat is also attractive to red fox, a great hunter of mice. Fox are active year-round but mostly at night. There numbers may be decreasing as the adaptable coyotes increase their territories.

Insects

Nearly everyone can recognize the banded woolly bears which are frequently seen crossing the towpath in September and October. This caterpillar has gained a reputation that far exceeds its very modest adult moth form. People try to predict the severity of winter by the size of its band, and thousands gather to honor it at the annual Woolly Bear Festival in Vermilion, Ohio.

You see the woolly bears out and about in the fall because they

Woolly Bear

are searching for secure places in which to hide throughout the winter months. The woolly bear grows up to be a small, inconspicuous, yellowish tiger moth.

White-marked tussock moths are also more noticeable as caterpillars than in their adult form. You recognize them by their long tuffs of hair all over their small bodies. Like very tiny, unkempt, furry animals, they sport cream-colored tuffs on their backs and longer black hairs projecting from head and tail ends. They're commonly seen in summer feeding on tree leaves, and one of the best spots to find them is just south of Peninsula along the towpath. The tussock moths use a clever technique to move from one feeding spot to another. They "parachute" by lowering themselves on a silk thread. The next gust of wind then blows the little creature a relatively great distance.

While you'll most likely notice the woolly bears and other caterpillars at your feet, overhead you can find the multi-celled nests of the bald-faced hornets. Watch for these nests hanging from tree branches; they are most obvious when the leaves are off the trees. The nests are gray and made of a papery material. The interior is layer upon layer of small cells, which at one time housed larvae of the hornets. Any remaining larvae die off in winter, while the queen hornet overwinters elsewhere. Adult bald-faced hornets are black, with light markings on the face, thorax, and end of the abdomen.

Reptiles

Three different snakes find the Towpath Trail and its surroundings compatible to their life styles, though sometimes risky as well. Snakes sunning themselves on the dry bright limestone surface of the path sometimes fall victim to bicycle wheels. Their more common predator, hawks, watch for them out in the open fields.

Common garter snakes are the most prevalent snakes of open fields such as the farm fields near the path. They can be a help to farmers, as they feed on both mice and insect pests. You're likely to just catch a glimpse of the garter snake or hear it moving off through the brush alongside the trail. They are harmless, but can bite if handled.

While garter snakes can be as long as 36 inches, brown snakes are smaller, usually no longer than a foot. They prefer to stay close to the protection of fallen trees, wood piles, or rock piles. They are brownish, with two black-dotted parallel stripes along their backs.

You can sometimes see ringneck snakes in the floodplain forests bordering the river, though they tend to be quite secretive and hide under logs or in loose bark. This snake is very distinctive, with a bright yellowish orange neck ring and bright orange underbelly.

Amphibians

Both the red-backed and two-lined salamanders live in this region of the valley. Red-backed salamanders are completely terrestrial, living out their lives on land, frequenting moist, decaying logs and other forest litter. They are one of the valley's most common amphibians, but are seldom seen because of their preference for hiding under logs and rocks. The two-lined, however, is found along or in fresh water streams.

Two-Lined Salamander

The shallow depressions along the Furnace Run stream bottom are good places to look for this salamander. They are very quick, darting in and out of the shelter of creek rocks, foraging for aquatic meals.

Both these salamanders have no lungs, but instead breathe through their thin, moist skin. Though they seem primitive and far-removed from any life form we are more familiar with, these tiny creatures have rather elaborate mating rituals, and the female red-backed salamanders are known to curl around and guard their clutches of eggs until the miniature hatchlings appear.

Winter

Winter is a time to discover nature's galleries—not those inside a warm museum, but the galleries designed by bark beetles and black carpenter ants. These beetles are also known as engraver beetles for their ability to carve long channels, or galleries, along the cambium layer of a tree trunk, just under the bark. The main gallery, of uniform width, is carved by the adult beetle, an insect only 1/8 inch long. Larval offspring carve the side galleries, radiating out from the main channel. These side channels increase in width, correlating to the growing larvae. Each separate species of bark beetle creates a pattern of these galleries characteristic of that species.

Bark Beetle Galleries

Bark beetles usually enter weak, dying, or dead trees, so they play a role in the breaking down of dead wood. The beetles' galleries can also allow for the entrance of fungi which rot the bark. It was in Ohio, in 1930, that foresters discovered that a fungus, later called Dutch elm disease, was rapidly killing the American elm trees, treasured for their beauty. The disease spread throughout the east, killing most of the elms. The culprit transporting the disease spores was the European elm bark beetle, carried to the United States in European elm logs, imported for their veneer.

Winter is also the time to look for vines which may be obscured by the thick greenery of other seasons. One vine that is most conspicuous in winter is wild cucumber. The small inedible fruit is covered with weak spines, like edible cucumbers, but this fruit then dries into a lightweight, papery shell. You will notice this vine draping over bare winter branches, its string of dried fruits waving gently in the wind.

Other vines to look for include grapes, moonseed, and greenbriers. Greenbrier stems are covered with stout prickles and this vine grows into almost impenetrable tangles, giving the plant the common names of tramps' troubles and blasphemy vine. These tangles provide cover for deer, rabbits, and catbirds.

Wild Cucumber

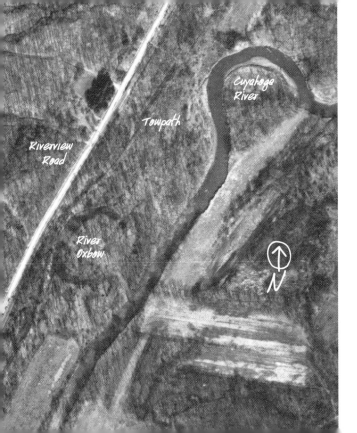

Riverview Road

Towpath

Cuyahoga River

River oxbow

N

Topography

From the vantage point of the trail you can observe two elements of the valley topography: a river oxbow to the east and exposed rock outcrops to the west. The oxbow lies east of the Towpath Trail between Milestone 25 and Milestone 26. The river meanders back and forth as it has for ages. The oxbow was formed when the energy of the river skipped straight across a meander, cutting off the curve and eventually separating it, leaving it as a half-moon shaped little pond (the oxbow name derives from the U-shaped part of an ox yoke). This oxbow lies close to the path and is filled with water most of the year. Wood ducks and mallards find that its calm and protected water makes a good resting spot.

When the leaves are off the trees, looking to the west at about this same half-way point along this section of the trail, you can see the Berea sandstone and Mississippian age shales exposed along the railroad cut. In winter the moisture oozing from the hills forms ice sculptures which hang from the stone.

Furnace Run, a major tributary of the Cuyahoga River, flows under a Towpath Trail bridge just north of Hunt Farm Visitor Information Center. Docile looking on a summer's day, Furnace Run can nonetheless flood rapidly; it has a very steep gradient, dropping 560 feet in 10.4 miles. Looking east from the bridge over the stream, you can barely see the point where it flows into the Cuyahoga River. The joining of the two floodplains forms a spacious broadening of the valley floor which is most obvious when approaching Hunt Farm by road. Early farmers found the place well suited for farming, with its flood-enriched soils and level ground, and to this day the land grows corn for man and beast.

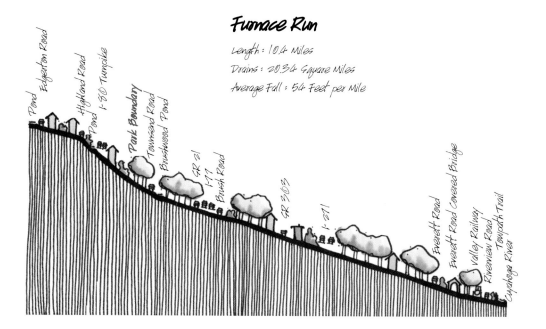

Furnace Run

Length : 10.4 Miles

Drains : 20.34 Square Miles

Average Fall : 54 Feet per Mile

I go to Nature to be soothed and healed,
and to have my senses put in tune once more.

John Burroughs

BUILD IT AND
THEY WILL COME

From Hunt Farm to Ira Road, today's landscape along the 1 3/4 miles of Towpath Trail is largely beaver-created. In the 1970s, the abandoned towpath was thickly overgrown. Part of it had served as a driveway to a house located north of Ira Road. Debris from a car repair shop littered the wet fields east of Riverview Road. A gravel mining operation behind the trailer park left acres of disturbed land between the river and the canal. Then in the late 1970s, after the establishment of Cuyahoga Valley National Recreation Area, beavers began to move into the area, transforming the low lying meadows into beaver ponds and rich wetland habitat.

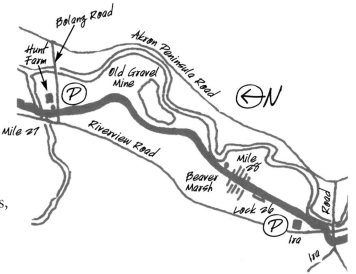

Car Repair Shop on Riverview Road
(Present Location of Beaver Marsh) c. 1915

clean-up

The National Park Service purchased and reseeded the gravel operation, then purchased and removed the car repair shop. In 1984 the Portage Trail Group of the Sierra Club organized a cleanup in the newly flooded beaver marsh. Tons of car parts, bed springs, household fixtures, and miscellaneous discards were hauled out and properly disposed. This was the first of many volunteer and park staff cleanups to take place in the valley. Removing the heaps of discarded items from ravines and house sites eliminated eyesores and aided the natural restoration process.

Near Ira Road, the first beavers built a substantial dam across the canal itself, but a break in the canal towpath allowed water to flow out to the east. The beavers continued to gather sticks and mud and extended their damming in a large 300-foot long arch away from the towpath and towards the river. At the beaver marsh, you see today what appears to be the banks of a natural pond but is actually the constructed and constantly maintained earthworks defining the beavers' watery world. The pond is fed by a small stream coming from the west, providing enough water to keep the pond deep enough for the beavers all year. The National Park Service has bridged the gap in the towpath with a boardwalk and observation platforms, making it possible to observe the beavers and their work at close hand.

Beaver-Chewed Stump

Since building that first dam, the expanding beaver family spread to the north and east. Young beavers stay with the parents until their second year, then are encouraged to move out and establish their own lodge and territory. Therefore, after the first dam was constructed, a second one appeared about 50 yards north, again across the canal. This is an exceptionally well-constructed dam, a "textbook example" of beaver construction, built

with the center of the dam slightly upstream of the ends. This arch shape is known by two-legged engineers to be inherently stronger, better able to support the force of the water behind it. In recent years other dams and lodges have been built, both in the canal and to either side. In the late 1990s, it was estimated that 15 to 18 beavers inhabited the area between Hunt Farm and Ira Road. The exact locations of their active lodges may change from year to year, but chances are very good that you will see beaver activity in this area somewhere along the canal.

Wetlands are among the richest and most productive of habitats because they are very good at capturing the sun's energy and recycling it in the form of plant and animal life. A most extraordinary facet of nature's way is that the beaver, in simply creating a suitable pond habitat for its own needs, creates a habitat that in turn invites many other forms of life to flourish. Of bird species alone, there are at least 65 different birds nesting in this wetland area. Five hundred nineteen different plants have been identified in the wetlands, along the towpath, and into the surrounding fields and forests near the path.

Take some time here. Return again and again. In all seasons and at all times of day you will find something happening. Water lilies cover the marsh in the summer like a Monet painting. Jewelweed crowds in upon the trail, and orioles flash their brilliant orange as they fly to nests suspended from sycamore branches. At dawn and dusk the beavers are out feeding and making repairs to the dams. In winter the great cycle of life does not stop but only rests, preparing for the surge of spring and another round of marsh life.

Wetland Habitat

Green Heron   Willows   Bluegill   Muskrat   Carp   Baltimore Oriole   Yellow

Iris   Waterlily   Beaver   Barn Swallow   Tree Swallow   Wood Ducks   Cattail   Dragonfly

Birds

Birders love this area. Within a short stroll, there are several different habitats or mini-habitats: the open water of the pond, cattail marsh edges, the river, brushy areas, fields, deciduous trees, and conifers. Of the many birds that it is possible to see here, eight are introduced here, each one taking its place in the complexity of the marsh.

One of the first birds to return to the beaver marsh in early spring is the tree swallow. This swallow's shiny blue-green back and pure white undersides are striking, especially in bright sunshine. It's nearly impossible to fix this bird in the sight of binoculars, and so it is best to just enjoy its swift flight pattern as it circles and veers over open water snatching insects from the air. Tree swallows are cavity nesters, selecting old woodpecker holes or other cavities in trees and buildings.

Birders at Beaver Marsh

In May, around Mothers' Day, you may begin to notice Baltimore orioles taking their places along the Towpath Trail. The male's rich, melodious whistle brings attention to this bright orange and black bird which prefers open woodland and riparian trees such as the tall sycamores lining the canal. Orioles are best known for their unique nests. The female, less dramatically colored in olive and yellow, weaves a hanging, pouch shaped nest by using plant fibers, hairs, and even yarn. Often you can find the nest by following the male in its flight. Orioles glean trees for caterpillars, and don't mind the hairy or spiny ones like those of tussock moths or gypsy moths.

Baltimore Oriole

Warbling vireos are tiny birds (5") that are more often heard than seen. They too frequent the sycamores and elms along the water's edge. The males sing endlessly, a simple, "warbling" melody, often from a tree top. While the vireo is a more solitary bird, cedar waxwings are noticeable because they are never alone. Their twittering noises may draw your attention to a treetop where the waxwings have gathered before taking off in a flurry. These small, sleek, crested birds travel in groups to feast on berries or insects. They are sociable, and have been seen passing berries back and forth, or passing a feather or insect during courtship. They have even been known to get drunk on fermented berry juices. Cedar waxwings actually have tiny drops of bright red wax which forms on the tips of their secondary wing feathers; the function of this wax is not known. Listen for the very high pitched lisping sound waxwings make while feeding.

Cedar Waxwing

Green Heron

Many Cuyahoga valley visitors are familiar with the great blue heron, one of our largest birds, standing as tall as 4 feet. The green heron is a smaller relative, about 17 inches long. It can be seen at very close range when it is intent on stalking for fish or frogs in the shallow water of the canal. Green herons let out an awkward squawk if disturbed. The sora and Virginia rail are chickenlike birds which stalk through cattails and grasses in the marshy areas. They do not like to fly, and they do not like to be seen; they give away their presence only by making strange grunts and whinnies.

Wood Ducks

These birds are declining in northeast Ohio due to the draining of wetlands, so it is quite significant that rails are consistently found in these marshes. The male wood duck's rainbow coloring makes it one of our most beautiful ducks. It has a red-orange eye set in an iridescent green and violet head; a line of yellow outlines its mottled beak; its black and white throat is set off against a warmly chestnut chest; indigo blue wing tips fold back over his black back above soft ivory sides. The female may be seen in early summer paddling down the canal with a long trail of youngsters behind her. Wood ducks are named so because they truly are forest birds, nesting in hollow trees.

Flowers

At least 500 different plants have been identified in the area along the Towpath Trail from Ira Road to the beaver marsh. Two of the most common and widespread (occurring throughout the valley) are jewelweed and wingstem. Jewelweeds grow abundantly in moist soil along the canal. The irregularly shaped flowers are usually yellow, sometimes with red-brown dots. Jewelweed is also known as touch-me-not. To find out why, check one out in late summer when its seeds are well-developed. Reach out to pick the swollen, slender green capsules and watch what happens. It's okay to nibble the small brown seeds inside the capsule—they have a butternutty taste. Common names often help us to recognize a plant. Such is the case with wingstem. Wingstem is a tall plant with yellow, daisy-like flowers. It grows abundantly along the path, flowering in late summer and fall. The way you can tell this flower from other composites is that the upper part of the stem is "winged" with thin ridges running along the stem sides.

Wingstem

Another common plant is yellow sweet clover. Clovers are in the pea family, and this clover has tiny yellow flowers resembling pea blossoms. It grows in old fields and disturbed sites, reaching 2 to 5 feet in height. The leaves have a pleasant, summery hay fragrance.

A plant with considerable notoriety is great ragweed. A rough looking plant, it grows up to 15 feet tall, and its tiny, unspectacular flowers release the pollen that is largely responsible for hay fever. Another giant of the trailside is great angelica. This plant resembles an enormously overgrown parsley plant, and is indeed in the parsley family. This parsley, however, unlike the snippets you get on

115

your dinner plate, grows to 7 feet tall by summertime and has tiny white flowers in round clusters, 3 to 10 inches wide. The thick stem is purplish. This plant is unmistakable and grows rapidly in the wet meadows near the canal.

In contrast to the unkempt ragweed and oversized great angelica, the Canada lily is an exquisite and much rarer plant. A few isolated lilies can be found growing along the Towpath Trail in mid-summer. This lily grows 2 to 5 feet tall and bears nodding 2 to 4-inch wide flowers, either yellow or rich red. The Canada lily is a native to this area and grows throughout eastern United States and Canada.

Three plants grow in the marsh itself and are easy to identify. Fragrant water lilies are the white-flowered plants which float on the surface of the marsh water. Like the beavers which author/naturalist Hope Ryden studied and wrote about in Lily Pond, the beavers in this marsh rely on the lilies for food. In the fullness of summer, a beaver will pick a large round leaf, use its forepaws to roll it up, then munch away. Ryden observed that beavers

Fragrant Water Lilies

also dig up the lilies' rhizomes or rooted stems for winter food.

Spatterdock grows along with the fragrant water lilies. It is also a lily, but its flower is more cuplike and is bright, glossy yellow. Female red-winged blackbirds hop across the plants' large leaves searching for insects to feed to their young.

Cattails are unmistakable and very common in marshes in the valley. The soft brown spikes are the female flowers of the plant; the male flowers grow above the brown spike and are tiny and yellowish. Cattails are edible—native Americans and early colonists made meal from the starchy roots. The young shoots are edible as well as immature flower stalks which can be boiled and enjoyed like corn-on-the-cob. Cattails provide excellent shelter for nesting marsh birds such as red-winged blackbirds, and muskrats use the stems in their mounded houses.

Trees

Aspen is a favorite food of beaver. In fact, some naturalists believe that it is the depletion of aspens in an area that causes beavers to move elsewhere. Both big-toothed and quaking aspens grow near the towpath. Aspens need sunshine to thrive and are known as a pioneer tree species, one the first to grow in areas which have been disturbed or cleared. The quaking or trembling nature of their leaves results from the fact that each leaf is attached to the stem by a flattened, flexible leafstalk. Aspens are closely related to cottonwoods which are also abundant along the river and canal.

"Elderberry pie" evokes an image of grandmothers, big warm kitchens, and delicious aromas. Today's bakers may not wish to fuss with the tiny berries, but the results are still well worth the effort. Raw, the berries have an unpleasant taste, and the other parts of the plant can cause digestive upsets, but cooked berries make delicious jams and pies. The elder shrubs grow in the moist soils along the canal and produce clusters of purplish-black fruits.

Mammals

Three out of the five most notable mammals in this section of trail live in wetland habitats. Beaver, muskrat, and mink all make their homes in or near the water. Beaver certainly are in the spotlight here, for they actually create or alter the ponds and connecting channels to suit their needs.

Beaver

Of all the places along the canal, here you have the best chance of observing beaver at close range. As they are nocturnal, the best time to observe them is before dawn or after dusk. You might first sight a beaver by spotting the "V" shape of the wake it makes when swimming. Even more likely, the beaver will sense your presence and startle you with a sharp, resounding whap of its flat tail on the water's surface, a warning given just before it dives.

Beaver construct and constantly repair their dams using sticks, mud, and sometimes rocks and available debris. Their lodges are similarly constructed of mud and sticks and small logs. A dry chamber, hollowed out above the water line, provides snug living quarters for a beaver family. Chips from the downing of trees make a fine, dry bedding for the beaver. For safety from predators, beaver have underwater entrance/exit tunnels.

Even if you do not see beavers, chances are good that you will see signs of their activities. As they drag branches from one place to another, they develop "haul trails" evidenced by drag marks. Large wood chips and pointed tree stumps give away their construction activities. Beaver tooth marks on the tree stumps are 1/8 to 1/4 inch wide. In the wintertime, clumps of branches placed in the water near the lodge, forming a winter food cache, indicate an active lodge. Two to four baby beaver are born in the spring and stay with the family until they are two years old.

These fascinating, highly adaptive creatures were hunted relentlessly for their furs in the 1700s and 1800s. They were extirpated from Ohio, but migrated back into the state in 1936, entered the Cuyahoga valley in the 1970s, and now are once again thriving throughout the state.

Muskrat

A muskrat swimming in the marsh or canal can be easily mistaken for a beaver, but differs by being much smaller and having a long, naked, rat-like tail, flattened side to side. Muskrat also build houses in the marsh, but these are smaller than beaver lodges and are built of matted vegetation on shore, in shallow water, or even on top of a beaver lodge. Muskrat and beaver coexist in the marsh without difficulty.

A flying mammal sounds like something from a cartoon, like a cow with wings. But bats distinguish themselves by being the only mammal that truly flies. A double membrane of skin turns the bat's hand into an effective wing. Two species of bats live in the Cuyahoga valley: little brown bats (in the genus *Myotis*) and big

Big Brown Bat

brown bats (in the genus *Eptesicus*). The little brown bats are colonial. They are the ones most likely seen flying erratically over the beaver marsh at night in search of insect food. Bats' eyes are nearly useless. They locate their flying food by echolocation, a type of sonar system, which allows them to fly in total

darkness. Hollow trees and barns serve as roosting places. If you are fortunate to find one of their roosts, you can observe them departing at dusk as if on cue, one after another. They feed during the night and return to roost before dawn.

Weasels, closely related to minks, are shaped similarly with a long, slender body. The longtail weasel is rare in the Cuyahoga valley. Weasels are a rich brown color, with whitish underparts. They eat small mammals such as mice and voles.

Coyotes have only recently found their way into the Cuyahoga valley. Due to the lack of records from the period of white settlement in Ohio, it is unclear whether or not coyotes were historically found here. In earlier times they may have been kept out of the entire northeast by wolves aggressively defending their territories. They now inhabit all the western, southwestern, and midwestern states, and are known to be as far northeast as Vermont.

Coyotes have been seen and heard at the Special Events Site, just west of the beaver marsh, and on occasion can be heard from the Towpath Trail. They are canids, related to dogs, foxes, and wolves. You know you've seen a coyote if you spot an animal that resembles a medium-sized German shepherd, but strikes you as not being a domestic dog—its nose is more pointed, tail is bushy, and it carries its tail down when running.

Although the sight and sound of coyotes seems so wild, they are really quite adapted to living near inhabited areas and because of that have

managed to increase their numbers in spite of being aggressively hunted. Coyotes have in the past gained notoriety, being blamed (often unfairly) for livestock losses. In the Cuyahoga valley they are protected from being hunted. Here they feed on road-kill deer, rabbits, and small rodents in farm fields. They are the only predator in the valley capable of killing small deer or fawns.

Insects

Summer in the marsh brings out a colorful collection of delicate damselflies and dragonflies. These wispy creatures, floating nearly weightlessly over the water, are actually voracious predators, keeping mosquitoes and midges

from taking over the marsh. Dragonflies and damselflies have been on Earth over 300 million years. They witnessed the appearance and disappearance of dinosaurs. Today, 5,000 species live throughout the world, with 450 in North America. The various colors and patterned wings of these insects inspire their common names: ten-spotted dragonfly, green-jacket skimmer, blackwinged damselfly, violet dancer damselfly, civil bluet damselfly.

At rest, dragonflies generally hold their wings outstretched, while damselflies hold theirs together above their bodies. Dragonflies enjoy the sun and may be found at rest on the surface of the towpath itself. Both dragonflies and damselflies are aquatic in their nymphal stage of life and are predacious both as nymphs underwater and adults above the water. Most people are familiar with them as adult insects, however fishermen may recognize the nymphs which become meals for young fish.

Dragonflies share the air above the water— each taking a certain altitude for their hunting space. The ten-spotted dragonfly (also known as the twelve-spotted skimmer) has the five-foot level. The ten-spotted is easy to identify by its dark spots on gauzy, many-veined wings. They are strong, fast flyers. They can be seen at rest on lily pads and small bushes at the edges of the beaver marsh.

Green-jacket dragonflies, also in the skimmer family, are sometimes called green clearwings. Both common names help describe them: the face, thorax, and abdomen are bright green,

Black-Winged Damselfly

and the wings are clear. They can be found along the edges of open marshes. This dragonfly, like other dragonfly species, helps to maintain a well-balanced ecosystem by feeding on a wide variety of smaller insects.

Damselflies are very slender, delicate looking creatures. The 1 to 1 1/4-inch civil bluets have light blue bodies with small, black markings. The violet dancer males are violet-bodied with clear wings. Females are dark brown. They are very common and may often be seen flying in tandem over the marsh.

A slightly larger relative of these two delicate denizens of the marsh is the black-winged damselfly.

The male of this species is metallic green with solid dark wings. Females are less spectacular, with brown bodies and one white spot on the wing tip. The black-winged damselfly is butterfly-like in its flight, but the males will defend their territory with obvious displays.

Northern Water Snake

Reptiles

This section of canal is one of several that deserve the nickname "turtle alley." In many ways turtles do not resemble other reptiles, however they do share the characteristic that they control their body temperature by behav-

ioral means—all turtles enjoy basking in the sun, and none more so than the numerous painted turtles in the canal. On warm, sunny days you can be assured of seeing painted turtles lined up on floating logs in shallow parts of the canal, often overlapping each other like shingles. Once disturbed, though, they all take

quickly to the safety of the water. Compared to painted turtles, snapping turtles, or "snappers," are more solitary and threatening in appearance. They can grow as long as 3 feet and though they appear heavy and slow, they can attack prey with amazing speed, and you do not want to be that prey.

The most common snake along the Towpath Trail is the northern water snake. It is frequently seen here, swimming in the marsh or canal or basking, draped over shrubs along the boardwalk. It is an excellent swimmer and often catches its meal of frogs or fish underwater. These snakes range in length from 22 to 53 inches!

Both green frogs and bullfrogs are very common in the canal and beaver ponds. Both have the habit of resting by floating in the open water with only their bulgy eyes above the water's surface Bullfrogs generally are larger than green frogs.

Northern leopard frogs begin life in ponds and marshes, but as adults they venture further from water than do green frogs and bullfrogs. Leopard frogs are most active at night, but if you should startle one during the day, it will flee in a zigzag course, heading for water.

Red Squirrel

Red squirrels are the smallest and most lively of squirrels found in the Cuyahoga River valley. Naturalist Olaus J. Murie accurately described them as "vivacious." They are reddish brown with pure white underbellies and an outline around each eye, making them look very bright-eyed. In the winter, you might find their tracks going from tree to tree.

You can also look for their middens, or piles of pine cone seeds, where they store other cones for later feeding. Red squirrels build two kinds of nests, an outside nest of twigs and grasses, and an inside nest in an old flicker hole or other tree cavity. A red squirrel will quickly grab a pine cone, scamper up to a tree limb, chatter at you loudly for intruding, then nibble the cone rapidly like a human hurriedly eating corn-on-the-cob.

Both beaver and muskrat are awake and active throughout winter. When there is ice on the ponds, beaver will remain in their lodges or move about below the ice, reaching their food cache from underneath. On a very cold day you might see a thin plume of vapor rising from the top of their lodge, indicating warm life within.

Muskrat and beaver are frequently found in the same pond. Muskrat houses are smaller than beaver lodges and are built of matted vegetation on shore, in shallow water, or even on top of a beaver lodge. Muskrat also build food shelters or feeding platforms, sometimes on top of ice, with a plunge hole like beavers use to reach the water below the ice.

Topography

Between Hunt Farm and Ira Road the valley floor (flood plains and terraces) is as wide as any section of the valley (about 3/5 of a mile) yet the valley width at 1000-foot elevation is only 3.5 miles.

It is here, in the area of wide river terraces, that lie the well drained loamy soils which overlay glacial deposits of sand and gravel. The glacial deposits have been mined in many areas. One of the most conspicuous quarries, now Indigo Lake, can be found by following the Hale Farm connector trail about 1/4 mile west from the Towpath Trail. This lake, unlike most other lakes and ponds in the valley, is not fed by surface water—its primary source is ground water. It is the constant flow from springs and seeps located well below the surface that keeps the lake full.

The northern end of this section of trail lies in the broad, maturing valley of Furnace Run, a major tributary of the Cuyahoga River. However, from Hunt Farm south to Ira Road, there are only two very minor creeks flowing into the valley from the east. These little waterways are captured by the canal depression and provide water for beaver ponds.

I like trees because they seem more resigned to the way they have to live than other things do.

Willa Cather

BENEATH THE BIG TREES

Between Ira Road and Bath Road, the Ohio & Erie Canal is no longer evident except for three sandstone "monuments" to the canal era—the west walls of Locks 24 and 25, and a spillway foundation near Lock 24. This section of trail is the same length as the section north of here, but differs greatly—it is close to Riverview Road and has no obvious canal depression. Also, the connection between the historic canal and the Cuyahoga River is less obvious, as Riverview Road lies largely in the old canal bed and separates the Towpath Trail from the river. What does help us get our towpath bearings are the very large old trees which line today's path and help mark the location of the old canal.

Because of Riverview Road's location, the Ohio & Erie Canal Towpath Trail does not lie on the historic towpath. The towpath was always located between the canal and the river where you now find Riverview Road. At times you are walking in the canal itself and at other times you are on the berm, or "heel-path." You can still get an idea where the canal was by locating the lock walls and then sighting along the row of largest sycamore trees. Farther north of the lock walls, at the corner of Riverview and Ira Roads, you can stand on the Towpath Trail at the southwest corner of the intersection and look to the northeast, diagonally across the intersection, to see where the canal resumes and still holds water. Draw an imaginary line from the big sycamores on the northeast corner to the big

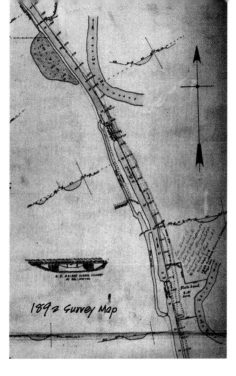

1892 Survey Map

sycamores near you on the southwest corner to see where the canal used to be.

The Valley Railway tracks closely parallel the Towpath Trail. West of the tracks and up the hillsides, lies 500 acres of fields and forest. This is the site of the historic Botzum family farm, one of the first farms in the valley. The uplands of this farm are forested with some sizable mixed hardwoods. In the lowlands are small wetlands, one of which is visible from the Towpath Trail. These wetlands attract ducks and red-winged blackbirds in the spring and provide breeding places for amphibians.

The spillway between Locks 24 and 25 is unusual in that it serves both locks. What is left of it now has converted into a small stream bed with water flowing throughout most of the year. Just north of Lock 25, the little creek that is spanned by the path is actually the end of the old spillway. A wider wetland near here, squeezed between the trail and the railroad tracks, is probably the remains of the canal bed.

The distinctive natural attraction along this section of Towpath Trail is the woodland itself, bordering and shading the trail from one end to the other. Fields to the west of the trail and intermittent wetland areas tucked in around the trail provide more, and varied, habitat for a diversity of species. Although the canal is long gone, you can still travel at a canal's pace and experience nature thriving beneath the big trees.

Birds

Of the six birds described here, one is known for its exceptionally striking color, and another for its exceptionally beautiful song. The scarlet tanager is surely one of our most beautiful birds: the male is flame-red with black wings and tail. Most tanagers are tropical birds, and this, our only tanager, brings the warmth of the tropics to the valley.

You may seldom see the wood thrush, but can nonetheless enjoy its presence through its singing. The wood thrush sings at dawn and dusk, like its more common relative, the American robin. Peterson's field guide

Scarlet Tanager

describes the song of the wood thrush as a "flutelike *ee-o-lay.*" It is the peaceful, unhurried song of summer. Wood thrushes, as you would guess, live in the woods, tending to remain low in the underbrush.

Most American robins leave the valley in the fall and return around March, coming north as they follow an average daily temperature of 37° F. They search for earthworms and insects in the soil, even under the intermittent snows that blanket the ground in early spring.

Gray catbirds are also more often heard than seen. The catbird's catlike mewing calls are frequently heard along the Towpath Trail. Catbirds, song sparrows, and yellow warblers frequent the multiflora rose bushes surrounding the Indian Mound parking lot.

Gray catbird

When the sun strikes the male indigo bunting, his intense indigo blue color is obvious. The female, however, is a dull brown. Indigo buntings sing vigorously from a treetop perch, and help us identify them by repeating each "word" twice, like "sweet-sweet," "chew-chew," "tweet, tweet," singing the paired phrases at different pitches.

At only one point along this stretch does the trail come close to the Cuyahoga River— near the remains of the Lock 25 west wall. Take a moment to look across the road towards the river. A belted kingfisher sometimes perches above the river, watching below for a meal. Kingfishers are solitary birds and are found throughout the valley

Belted Kingfisher

near streams and ponds. They are known to favor a particular perch from which they can dive for fish.

Kingfishers are blue-gray, with a scruffy double crest. They have a white collar and band of blue-gray on the chest. The female also has a chestnut band across the chest and chestnut along her flanks, making her more colorful than her mate—a rarity among North American birds. Kingfishers build horizontal burrows in the riverbanks for nesting.

Listen for the kingfisher's rattling call as it flies along the river. It will dive for fish then take its catch to a perch, toss it in the air, and swallow it head first.

Flowers

Of the flowering plants featured in this section, several take advantage of the small wetland patches and wet woods, while others grow along the drier edges of the path. Jewelweed can be found along nearly the entire length of Towpath Trail and grows rampantly in the moist places here. Swamp buttercup and swamp rose mallow also favor wet places but are much less common. Both have showy, beautiful flowers—shiny yellow flowers on the buttercup and large, 4 to 6-inch wide pink flowers on the swamp rose mallow. Look for the swamp rose mallow in the summertime. It is a type of hibiscus, very showy and tall, growing to the west of the trail in the wetland areas.

Swamp Rose Mallow

Another mallow, Indian mallow or velvetleaf, is native to India. In Ohio it grows in disturbed areas and at trailsides and roadsides. This mallow bears 1 inch wide yellow flowers on a tall plant with heart-shaped, velvety leaves.

Three other common summertime flowers are all in the composite family. Chicory is a common roadside plant which has found its way to North America from Europe. It now graces rough edges with its sky-blue flowers. In Europe, chicory is cultivated for its roots which are roasted and ground up as a coffee substitute or additive.

Chickory

Oxeye Daisy

The oxeye daisy is a white-and-yellow-flowered relative of chicory, equally common and familiar. It usually has one single composite type flower (1 to 2 inches wide) at the top of a 1 to 3-foot stem. Common boneset on the other hand has flat-topped clusters of many tiny dull-white flowers. The stem appears to be growing right through the opposite, joined leaves. Early herbalists used it to treat coughs and fevers. It may have gained its name from the fact that one of those fevers was a flu causing severe body aches and was known as breakbone fever.

Trees

Eastern cottonwoods and sycamores of impressive size shade the Towpath Trail from Ira Road to Bath Road. One of the old sycamores measures 18 feet in circumference. Early settlers, however, found sycamores measuring up to 40 feet around. This gives the tree the distinction of being the largest in girth of all deciduous hardwoods in North America. Many sycamores, as they age, become hollowed out from heart rot. They can continue to grow in girth, however, and the hollows provide great roosting and nesting places for opossums, raccoons, and chimney swifts. Folklore tells of hollowed trunks having been used as winter or storm refuges for man as well.

While a sycamore can live to 500 or 600 years, eastern cottonwoods begin deteriorating after only 70 or 80 years. Like sycamores, they grow quickly and do best in wet lowlands. They are not bothered by silt or periodic flooding. In early summer, clouds of white cotton float down from these tall trees—the numerous tufted seeds are dispersed by the wind and blown into windrows. All summer long, on breezy days, you can hear the papery rustling of the large coarse leaves.

Eastern Cottonwood

Mammals

White-tailed deer browse in the woodlands and fields here near the Towpath Trail just as they do throughout the rest of the valley. Their meals consist of twigs, fungi, grass, and

White-Tailed Fawn

acorns. In winter the deer gather and move in large groups, while in the spring and summer they live singly or in doe and fawn groups. The spotted coloration of the young fawns helps to camouflage them in the dappled sunlight of the forest.

Eastern gray squirrels are common throughout the valley and can be seen scrambling in the tall trees along the trail. Less common, but present, is the southern flying squirrel. You will have to venture out at night to see this nocturnal squirrel. Listen for faint twittering sounds in the trees to locate them.

Flying squirrels are equipped with a folded layer of loose skin along each

Flying squirrel

side of their bodies, stretching from front leg to hind leg. When outstretched, this skin fold allows the squirrels to glide from tree to tree in the dark forest, "flying" as much as 150 feet in each glide.

This area is also perfectly suited to eastern cottontail rabbits. Rabbits inhabit strips of forest near open areas and have adapted to suburban living. Cottontails stay hidden, hunkered down in the brush during the day, finding excellent use for the impenetrable brambles which hikers avoid.

The rabbits become active from early evening to late morning, feeding on lush green vegetation in the summer and on twigs and buds in the winter. Rabbits have many enemies and must be constantly wary. One effective species survival mechanism is their reproduction rate: a female may bear up to twenty young in a year, and some of the offspring will mate and give birth the same year.

Eastern cottontail

Insects

Summertime is the best time for learning more about the varied insects of the Towpath Trail. If you are interested in expanding your nature knowledge, why not begin to know the insects? There are plenty out there—over 88,600 species in North America alone! Insects are small and inhabit small habitats, so you can find many different species in one small area. Because each species prefers particular plants, learning the plants and their habitats can guide you in your insect discovery. There are five different insects that can be easily identified in this towpath area.

Green Darner

The green darner is a very large dragonfly (with a wingspan to 4 3/8 inches) which has earned the nicknames of "snake doctor" and "darning needle." It is big and fast, and can be seen flying over the fields near Indian Mound Trailhead, snatching mosquitoes, midges, and other insects from the air.

The Virginia ctenuchid moth is a small day-flying moth which frequents the goldenrod patches near Indian Mound Trailhead. These moths on close inspection are quite colorful, with metallic blue-green bodies and an orange-yellow head. They are often mistaken as wasps, which is a protective mechanism, warding off predators.

One of the most effective predacious insects along the path is the aptly named six-spotted green tiger beetle. Watch for the tiger beetle right on the Towpath Trail.

Rarely can you approach any closer than three feet, however, because this beetle is extremely wary and fast. This beetle has long legs, long antennae, and is a brilliant metallic green color with a purplish sheen. It also usually sports three to five white spots near its shiny rear.

Red admiral and question mark butterflies both prefer the open areas of the narrow floodplain forest here along the path. Nettles, which hikers prudently

Six-Spotted Green Tiger Be

avoid, are a favorite host plant of the red admirals. Red admirals are smaller than monarch butterflies, but share a similar mixture of colors: admirals have rich dark brown wings with a few white spots and an orange cross band on the forewings and orange margin on the hind wings.

Question mark butterflies are also orange and brown and have ragged wing edges tinged with pale lilac. The silvery "question mark" is located on the underside of the hind wing and can only be seen on close inspection. Question mark caterpillars feed on the leaves of host plants, including the many elms which grow near the trail. Adult question marks sip on sap and rotting fruit. They can become intoxicated if they imbibe fermented fruit.

Reptiles

Both common garter snakes and brown snakes can be found in the large fields near Indian Mound Trailhead and in grassy areas along the Towpath Trail. Brown snakes stay close to water or damp areas, feeding on earthworms, slugs, and snails. These snakes are small, nonaggressive, and like all snakes in the Cuyahoga valley, they are nonpoisonous. The young are born in August and are only 4 inches long, smaller than many earthworms. This is the only brown-colored snake with two rows of evenly placed black dots along its length. They must be highly adaptable, as they can be found both in wild places as well as in littered vacant city lots.

Amphibians

For many naturalists, there is no sweeter springtime song than the trilling of the American toad. While spring peepers and western chorus frogs move to the ponds as early as March, the toads begin calling for mates in warmer late April, about the time the grass greens up. You can hear them both day and night when the temperature rises above 60°F or so. Toads live in the wet woods along the Towpath Trail and migrate to shallow ponds or puddles to mate and lay eggs. Watch for thumbnail-sized toads as they leave the ponds and head back to the forest in June and July. Toads are extremely beneficial in maintaining the balance of the forest ecosystem, consuming as many as 10,000 insects in just three months.

Red-backed salamanders live in the moist places of the floodplain woodlands. Salamanders are amphibians—the first vertebrates to adapt to living on land.

American Toads

Unlike reptiles, however, amphibians have never fully divorced themselves from water and are vulnerable to dehydration, thus confining themselves to moist places.

Winter

Many signs of deer can be found in the winter. Herds of deer tend to confine themselves to a limited area with a maze of packed down trails which they use to reach food and escape from harm. Such an area is called a deer yard. Deer need to keep up their body temperature and conserve energy in winter. Finding food is a challenge, especially in deep snow. In such conditions, deer switch their diet from green plants to buds of deciduous trees and foliage of evergreens. Where deer populations are large, you can see evidence of their winter feeding, a "browse line"—the evergreens will be devoid of branches up to the height of the deer's reach.

Oval depressions of packed snow or packed grasses indicate deer beds. The familiar two-toed tracks will be around the bedding area, as well as the small dark oval pellets of scat. In late fall and early winter you can see a sign left by the males: they rub their antlers against tree trunks and shrubs, leaving characteristic scrape marks.

Antler Rub Marks

Topography

Yellow Creek slips under the Towpath Trail just north of Bath Road. It is about 10 miles long, about the same length as Furnace Run, and like Furnace Run, it flows to the Cuyahoga River from the west. Both streams originate at two of the highest elevations found along the west rim of the valley. The confluence of Yellow Creek and the river is just east of Riverview Road.

An abandoned river meander creates a big U-shaped wetland in the floodplain halfway between Ira Road and Bath Road.

This meander lies to the east of Riverview Road (opposite Lock 25) and is barely discernible even in the winter, as it is well obscured by dense vegetation.

Here at the southern end of the Towpath Trail in CVNRA, the path lies atop a valley floor which consists of 300-foot deep lake deposits and glacial debris which buried a much more ancient river valley. This burying, or veneering, has happened time after time over a period of a million years.

I only went out for a walk
and finally concluded to
stay out until sundown,
for going out, I found,
was really going in.

John Muir

Birds

Herons:
- ☐ Great Blue Heron (*Ardea herodias*)
- ☐ Great Egret (*Ardca alba*)
- ☐ Green Heron (*Butorides virescens*)

Geese & Ducks:
- ☐ American Black Duck (*Anas rubripes*)
- ☐ Canada Goose (*Branta canadensis*)
- ☐ Mallard (*Anas platyrhynchos*)
- ☐ Wood Duck (*Aix sponsa*)

Vultures & Hawks:
- ☐ American Kestrel (*Falco sparverius*)
- ☐ Broad-winged Hawk (*Buteo platypterus*)
- ☐ Cooper's Hawk (*Accipiter cooperii*)
- ☐ Red-shouldered Hawk (*Buteo lineatus*)
- ☐ Red-tailed Hawk (*Buteo jamaicensis*)
- ☐ Turkey Vulture (*Cathartes aura*)
- ☐ Wild Turkey (*Meleagris gallopavo*)

Rails & Coots:
- ☐ American Coot (*Fulica americana*)
- ☐ Sora (*Porzana carolina*)
- ☐ Virginia Rail (*Rallus limicola*)

Shorebirds & Gulls:
- ☐ American Woodcock (*Scolopax minor*)
- ☐ Herring Gull (*Larus argentatus*)
- ☐ Ring-billed Gull (*Larus delawarensis*)
- ☐ Killdeer (*Charadrius vociferus*)
- ☐ Spotted Sandpiper (*Actitus macularia*)

Doves:
- ☐ Mourning Dove (*Zenaida macroura*)
- ☐ Rock Dove (*Columba livia*)

Owls:
- ☐ Barred Owl (*Strix varia*)
- ☐ Eastern Screech Owl (*Otus asio*)
- ☐ Great Horned Owl (*Bubo virginianus*)

- ☐ Chimney Swift (*Chaetura pelagica*)
- ☐ Ruby-throated Hummingbird (*Archilochus colubris*)
- ☐ Belted Kingfisher (*Ceryle alcyon*)

Woodpeckers:
- ☐ Downy Woodpecker (*Picoides pubescens*)
- ☐ Hairy Woodpecker (*Picoides villosus*)
- ☐ Northern Flicker (*Colaptes auratus*)
- ☐ Pileated Woodpecker (*Dryocopus pileatus*)
- ☐ Red-bellied Woodpecker (*Melanerpes carolinus*)

Flycatchers:
- ☐ Acadian Flycatcher (*Empidonax virescens*)
- ☐ Eastern Kingbird (*Tyrannus tyrannus*)
- ☐ Eastern Phoebe (*Sayornis phoebe*)
- ☐ Eastern Wood Pewee (*Contopus virens*)
- ☐ Great Crested Flycatcher (*Myiarchus crinitus*)
- ☐ Willow Flycatcher (*Empidonax traillii*)

Vireos:

- ☐ Blue-headed Vireo *(Vireo solitarius)*
- ☐ Red-eyed Vireo *(Vireo olivaceus)*
- ☐ Warbling Vireo *(Vireo gilvus)*
- ☐ White-eyed Vireo *(Vireo griseus)*
- ☐ Yellow-throated Vireo *(Vireo flavifrons)*

Jays & Crows:

- ☐ American Crow *(Corvus brachyrhynchos)*
- ☐ Blue Jay *(Cyanocitta cristata)*

Swallows:

- ☐ Bank Swallow *(Riparia riparia)*
- ☐ Barn Swallow *(Hirundo rustica)*
- ☐ Northern Rough-winged Swallow *(Stelgidopteryx serripennis)*
- ☐ Tree Swallow *(Tachycineta bicolor)*
- ☐ Black-capped Chickadee *(Poecile atricapillus)*
- ☐ Tufted Titmouse *(Baeolophus bicolor)*
- ☐ White-breasted Nuthatch *(Sitta carolinensis)*

- ☐ Brown Creeper *(Certhia americana)*

Wrens:

- ☐ Carolina Wren *(Thryothorus ludovicianus)*
- ☐ House Wren *(Troglodytes aedon)*

Gnatcatchers & Kinglets:

- ☐ Blue-gray Gnatcatcher *(Polioptila caerulea)*
- ☐ Golden-crowned Kinglet *(Regulus satrapa)*
- ☐ Ruby-crowned Kinglet *(Regulus calendula)*

Thrushes:

- ☐ American Robin *(Turdus migratorius)*
- ☐ Eastern Bluebird *(Sialia sialis)*
- ☐ Veery *(Catharus fuscescens)*
- ☐ Wood Thrush *(Hylocichla mustelina)*

- ☐ Gray Catbird *(Dumetella carolinensis)*
- ☐ Cedar Waxwing *(Bombycilla cedrorum)*
- ☐ European Starling *(Sturnus vulgaris)*

Warblers:

- ☐ American Redstart *(Setophaga ruticilla)*

- ☐ Black-throated Green Warbler *(Dendroica virens)*
- ☐ Blue-winged Warbler *(Vermivora pinus)*
- ☐ Cerulean Warbler *(Dendroica cerulea)*
- ☐ Common Yellowthroat *(Geothlypis trichas)*
- ☐ Hooded Warbler *(Wilsonia citrina)*
- ☐ Louisiana Waterthrush *(Seiurus motacilla)*
- ☐ Ovenbird *(Seiurus aurocapillus)*
- ☐ Prothonotary Warbler *(Protonotaria citrea)*
- ☐ Yellow Warbler *(Dendroica petechia)*
- ☐ Yellow-breasted Chat *(Icteria virens)*
- ☐ Yellow-rumped Warbler *(Dendroica coronata)*
- ☐ Yellow-throated Warbler *(Dendroica dominica)*

- ☐ Scarlet Tanager *(Piranga olivacea)*
- ☐ Eastern Towhee *(Pipilo erythrophthalmus)*

Sparrows:

- ☐ American Tree Sparrow *(Spizella arborea)*
- ☐ Chipping Sparrow *(Spizella passerina)*
- ☐ Field Sparrow *(Spizella pusilla)*
- ☐ Fox Sparrow *(Passerella iliaca)*

- [ ] Song Sparrow *(Melospiza melodia)*
- [ ] Swamp Sparrow *(Melospiza georgiana)*
- [ ] White-crowned Sparrow *(Zonotrichia leucophrys)*
- [ ] White-throated Sparrow *(Zonotrichia albicollis)*
- [ ] Dark-eyed Junco *(Junco hyemalis)*
- [ ] Northern Cardinal *(Cardinalis cardinalis)*
- [ ] Rose-breasted Grosbeak *(Pheucticus ludovicianus)*
- [ ] Indigo Bunting *(Passerina cyanea)*
- [ ] Bobolink *(Dolichonyx oryzivorus)*

Blackbirds:
- [ ] Red-winged Blackbird *(Agelaius phoeniceus)*
- [ ] Common Grackle *(Quiscalus quiscula)*
- [ ] Eastern Meadowlark *(Sturnella magna)*
- [ ] Brown-headed Cowbird *(Molothrus ater)*

Orioles:
- [ ] Baltimore Oriole *(Icterus galbula)*
- [ ] Orchard Oriole *(Icterus spurius)*

Finches:
- [ ] American Goldfinch *(Carduelis tristis)*
- [ ] House Finch *(Carpodacus mexicanus)*
- [ ] House Sparrow *(Passer domesticus)*

 *Flowers*

Flowering March-May
- [ ] Bloodroot *(Sanguinaria canadensis)*
- [ ] Blue Cohosh *(Caulophyllum thalictroides)*
- [ ] Blue Flag *(Iris versicolor)*
- [ ] Blue Phlox *(Phlox divaricata)*
- [ ] Bluets *(Houstonia caerulea)*
- [ ] Buttercups *(Ranunculus spp.)*
- [ ] Cinquefoils *(Potentilla spp.)*
- [ ] Coltsfoot *(Tussilago farfara)*
- [ ] Common Arrowhead *(Sagittaria latifolia)*

- [ ] Common Boneset *(Eupatorium perfoliatum)*
- [ ] Common Dandelion *(Taraxacum officinale)*
- [ ] Common Dodder *(Cuscuta gronovii)*
- [ ] Cut-leaved Toothwort *(Dentaria laciniata)*
- [ ] Early Meadow Rue *(Thalictrum dioicum)*
- [ ] False Solomon's Seal *(Smilacina racemosa)*
- [ ] Fleabanes *(Erigeron spp.)*
- [ ] Foam Flower *(Tiarella cordifolia)*
- [ ] Forget-me-nots *(Myosotis spp.)*
- [ ] Garlic Mustard *(Alliaria petiolata)*
- [ ] Jack-in-the-Pulpit *(Arisaema triphyllum)*
- [ ] Large-flowered Trillium *(Trillium grandiflorum)*
- [ ] Marsh Marigold *(Caltha palustris)*
- [ ] Mayapple *(Podophyllum peltatum)*
- [ ] Pennsylvania Bitter Cress *(Cardamine pennsylvanica)*
- [ ] Purple Cress *(Cardamine douglassii)*
- [ ] Round-lobed Hepatica *(Hepatica americana)*
- [ ] Rue Anemone *(Anemonella thalictroides)*

- [ ] Sharp-lobed Hepatica (*Hepatica acutiloba*)
- [ ] Skunk Cabbage (*Symplocarpus foetidus*)
- [ ] Smooth Solomon's Seal (*Polygonatum biflorum*)
- [ ] Spring Beauty (*Claytonia virginica*)
- [ ] Squirrel Corn (*Dicentra canadensis*)
- [ ] Twinleaf (*Jeffersonia diphylla*)
- [ ] Violets (*Viola spp.*)
- [ ] Virginia Bluebell (*Mertensia virginica*)
- [ ] Wild Geranium (*Geranium maculatum*)
- [ ] Wild Ginger (*Asarum canadense*)
- [ ] Wild Leek (*Allium tricoccum*)
- [ ] Wild Strawberry (*Fragaria virginiana*)
- [ ] Yellow Iris (*Iris pseudacorus*)
- [ ] Yellow Trout Lily (*Erythronium americanum*)

Flowering June -July

- [ ] Beggar-ticks (*Bidens spp.*)
- [ ] Bindweeds (*Convolvulus spp.*)

- [ ] Bittersweet Nightshade (*Solanum dulcamara*)
- [ ] Black-eyed Susan (*Rudbeckia hirta*)
- [ ] Canada Lily (*Lilium canadense*)
- [ ] Cattails (*Typha spp.*)
- [ ] Chicory (*Cichorium intybus*)
- [ ] Common Evening Primrose (*Oenothera biennis*)
- [ ] Common Milkweed (*Asclepias syriaca*)
- [ ] Common Mullein (*Verbascum thapsus*)
- [ ] Common Periwinkle (*Vinca minor*)
- [ ] Common Ragweed (*Ambrosia artemisiifolia*)
- [ ] Common Teasel (*Dipsacus sylvestris*)
- [ ] Cow Parsnip (*Heracleum maximum*)
- [ ] Curled Dock (*Rumex crispus*)
- [ ] Dame's Rocket (*Hesperis matronalis*)
- [ ] Dogbanes (*Apocynum spp.*)
- [ ] Duckweed (*Lemna minor*)
- [ ] Giant Reed Grass (*Phragmites australis*)
- [ ] Goldenrods (*Solidago spp.*)

- [ ] Grapes (*Vitis spp.*)
- [ ] Great Angelica (*Angelica atropurpurea*)
- [ ] Great Ragweed (*Ambrosia trifida*)
- [ ] Green-headed Coneflower (*Rudbeckia laciniata*)
- [ ] Ground Ivy (*Glechoma hederacea*)
- [ ] Hawkweeds (*Hieracium spp.*)
- [ ] Heal All (*Prunella vulgaris*)
- [ ] Honeysuckles (*Lonicera spp.*)
- [ ] Horseweed (*Erigeron canadensis*)
- [ ] Japanese Knotweed (*Polygonum cuspidatum*)
- [ ] Loosestrifes (*Lysimachia spp.*)
- [ ] Moth Mullein (*Verbascum blattaria*)
- [ ] Tall Ironweed (*Vernonia gigantea*)
- [ ] Ox-eye Daisy (*Chrysanthemum leucanthemum*)
- [ ] Pale Touch-me-not (*Impatiens pallida*)
- [ ] Poison Hemlock (*Conium maculatum*)

- ☐ Poison Ivy (*Rhus radicans radicans*)
- ☐ Pokeweed (*Phytolacca americana*)
- ☐ Purple Dead Nettle (*Lamium purpureum*)
- ☐ Purple Loosestrife (*Lythrum salicaria*)
- ☐ Queen Anne's Lace (*Daucus carota*)
- ☐ Rattlesnake Root (*Prenanthes altissima*)
- ☐ Red Clover (*Trifolium pratense*)
- ☐ Rough Bedstraw (*Galium asprellum*)
- ☐ Soapwort (*Saponaria officinalis*)
- ☐ Spatterdock (*Nuphar variegatum*)
- ☐ Spotted Joe-Pye Weed (*Eupatorium maculatum*)
- ☐ Spotted Knapweed (*Centaurea maculosa*)
- ☐ Spotted Touch-me-not (*Impatiens capensis*)
- ☐ St. Johnsworts (*Hypericum spp.*)
- ☐ Stinging Nettle (*Urtica dioica*)
- ☐ Sunflowers (*Helianthus spp.*)
- ☐ Thistles (*Cirsium spp.*)
- ☐ Tick Trefoils (*Desmodium spp.*)

- ☐ Tickseeds (*Coreopsis spp.*)
- ☐ Trumpet Creeper (*Campsis radicans*)
- ☐ Velvetleaf (*Abutilon theophrasti*)
- ☐ Virgin's Bower (*Clematis virginiana*)
- ☐ Virginia Creeper (*Parthenocissus quinquefolia*)
- ☐ Virginia Knotweed (*Tovara virginiana*)
- ☐ Water Lilies (*Nymphaea spp.*)
- ☐ Wild Bergamot (*Monarda fistulosa*)
- ☐ Wild Cucumber (*Echinocystis lobata*)
- ☐ Wild Garlic (*Allium canadense*)
- ☐ Wild Yamroot (*Dioscorea villosa*)
- ☐ Wingstem (*Actinomeris alternifolia*)
- ☐ Yellow Sweet Clover (*Melilotus officinalis*)

Flowering August-September
- ☐ Asters (*Aster spp.*)
- ☐ Common Burdock (*Arctium minus*)

Non-Flowering
- ☐ Christmas Fern (*Polystichum acrostichoides*)

- ☐ Sensitive Fern (*Onoclea sensibilis*)
- ☐ Field Horsetail (*Equisetum arvense*)
- ☐ Scouring Rush (*Equisetum hiemale*)

Trees & Shrubs

- ☐ American Basswood (*Tilia americana*)
- ☐ American Beech (*Fagus grandifolia*)

Aspens:
- ☐ Bigtooth Aspen (*Populus grandidentata*)
- ☐ Quaking Aspen (*Populus tremuloides*)

Ashes:
- ☐ White Ash (*Fraxinus americana*)
- ☐ Red Ash (*Fraxinus pennsylvanica*)

- ☐ Black Cherry (*Prunus serotina*)
- ☐ Black Gum (*Nyssa sylvatica*)

- ☐ Black Locust (*Robinia pseudo-acacia*)
- ☐ Black Raspberry (*Rubus occidentalis*)
- ☐ Black Walnut (*Juglans nigra*)
- ☐ Blackberry (*Rubus allegheniensis*)
- ☐ Buttonbush (*Cephalanthus occidentalis*)
- ☐ Common Chokecherry (*Prunus virginiana*)
- ☐ Common Spicebush (*Lindera benzoin*)

Dogwoods:
- ☐ Flowering Dogwood (*Cornus florida*)
- ☐ Gray Dogwood (*Cornus racemosa*)

- ☐ Eastern Cottonwood (*Populus deltoides*)
- ☐ Eastern Hemlock (*Tsuga canadensis*)
- ☐ Elderberry (*Sambucus canadensis*)

Elms:
- ☐ American Elm (*Ulmus americana*)
- ☐ Slippery Elm (*Ulmus rubra*)

- ☐ European Alder Buckthorn (*Rhamnus frangula*)
- ☐ Hawthorns (*Crataegus spp.*)

- ☐ Ironwood (*Carpinus caroliniana*)

Maples:
- ☐ Box Elder (*Acer negundo*)
- ☐ Red Maple (*Acer rubrum*)
- ☐ Silver Maple (*Acer saccharinum*)
- ☐ Sugar Maple (*Acer saccharum*)

- ☐ Multiflora Rose (*Rosa multiflora*)

Oaks:
- ☐ Bur Oak (*Quercus macrocarpa*)
- ☐ Red Oak (*Quercus rubra*)
- ☐ White Oak (*Quercus alba*)

- ☐ Ohio Buckeye (*Aesculus glabra*)
- ☐ Sassafras (*Sassafras albidum*)

Sumacs:
- ☐ Smooth Sumac (*Rhus glabra*)
- ☐ Staghorn Sumac (*Rhus typhina*)

- ☐ Sycamore (*Platanus occidentalis*)
- ☐ Tuliptree (*Liriodendron tulipifera*)

- ☐ Viburnums (*Viburnum spp.*)
- ☐ Wild Crabapples (*Malus spp.*)
- ☐ White Pine (*Pinus strobus*)

Willows:
- ☐ Black Willow (*Salix nigra*)
- ☐ Crack Willow (*Salix fragilis*)
- ☐ Heart-leaved Willow (*Salix rigida*)
- ☐ Pussy Willow (*Salix discolor*)
- ☐ Sandbar Willow (*Salix exigua*)

- ☐ Witch Hazel (*Hamamelis virginiana*)

Mammals

Bats:
- ☐ Big Brown Bat (*Eptesicus fuscus*)
- ☐ Little Brown Bat (*Myotis lucifugus*)

- ☐ Beaver (*Castor canadensis*)

- ☐ Coyote *(Canis latrans)*
- ☐ Eastern Chipmunk *(Tamias striatus)*
- ☐ Eastern Cottontail *(Sylvilagus floridanus)*

Foxes:
- ☐ Gray Fox *(Urocyon cinereoargenteus)*
- ☐ Red Fox *(Vulpes vulpes)*

- ☐ Meadow Vole *(Microtus pennsylvanicus)*

Mice:
- ☐ White-footed Mouse *(Peromyscus leucopus)*
- ☐ Meadow Jumping Mouse *(Zapus hudsonius)*
- ☐ House Mouse *(Mus musculus)*

- ☐ Mink *(Mustela vison)*

Moles:
- ☐ Eastern Mole *(Scalopus aquaticus)*
- ☐ Hairy-tailed Mole *(Parascalops breweri)*
- ☐ Star-nosed Mole *(Condylura cristata)*

- ☐ Muskrat *(Ondatra zibethicus)*

- ☐ Norway Rat *(Rattus norvegicus)*
- ☐ Raccoon *(Procyon lotor)*

Shrews:
- ☐ Short-tailed Shrew *(Blarina brevicauda)*
- ☐ Smoky Shrew *(Sorex fumeus)*
- ☐ Masked Shrew *(Sorex cinereus)*

Squirrels:
- ☐ Eastern Fox Squirrel *(Sciurus niger)*
- ☐ Eastern Gray Squirrel *(Sciurus carolinensis)*
- ☐ Red Squirrel *(Tamiasciurus hudsonicus)*
- ☐ Southern Flying Squirrel *(Glaucomys volans)*

- ☐ Striped Skunk *(Mephitis mephitis)*
- ☐ Virginia Opossum *(Didelphis virginiana)*

Weasels:
- ☐ Least Weasel *(Mustela nivalis)*
- ☐ Longtail Weasel *(Mustela frenata)*

- ☐ White-tailed Deer *(Odocoileus virginianus)*
- ☐ Woodchuck *(Marmota monax)*

Insects

Moth Caterpillars:
- ☐ Banded Wooly Bear *(Pyrrharctia isabella)*
- ☐ Eastern Tent Caterpillar *(Malacosoma americanum)*
- ☐ Fall Webworm *(Hyphantria cunea)*

Aphidlike Insects:
- ☐ Aphids *(Aphididae spp.)*
- ☐ Meadow Spittlebug *(Philaenus spumarius)*

Earwigs:
- ☐ European Earwig *(Forficula auricularia)*

Diving Beetles and Water Bugs:
- ☐ Diving Beetles *(Dytiscus spp.)*
- ☐ Water Boatman *(Corixidae)*
- ☐ Water Strider *(Gerris remigis)*
- ☐ Wheel Bug *(Arilus cristatus)*
- ☐ Large Whirligig Beetles *(Dineutus spp.)*

Hopperlike Insects:
- ☐ Green Sharpshooters *(Draculacephalus spp.)*
- ☐ Scarlet-and-green Leafhopper *(Graphocephala coccinea)*

Plant Bugs:
- ☐ Green Stink Bug *(Acrosternum hilare)*
- ☐ Ambush Bugs *(Phymata spp.)*
- ☐ Harlequin Bug *(Murgantia histrionica)*
- ☐ Large Milkweed Bug *(Oncopeltus fasciatus)*
- ☐ Squash Bug *(Anasa tristis)*

Beetles:
- ☐ Bark Beetles *(Scolytus spp.)*
- ☐ Beautiful Tiger Beetle *(Cicindela formosa)*
- ☐ Black Ground Beetles *(Pterostichus spp.)*
- ☐ Brown Click Beetles *(Melanotus spp.)*
- ☐ Carrion Beetles *(Silpha spp.)*
- ☐ Caterpillar Hunter *(Calosoma scrutator)*
- ☐ Cottonwood Borer Beetle *(Plectrodera scalator)*
- ☐ Golden Tortoise Beetle *(Metriona bicolor)*
- ☐ Golden-haired Flower Longhorn Beetle *(Leptura chrysocoma)*
- ☐ Goldenrod Soldier Beetle *(Chauliognathus pennsylvanicus)*
- ☐ Japanese Beetle *(Popilla japonica)*
- ☐ June Bugs or May Beetles *(Phyllophaga spp.)*
- ☐ Larger Black Blister Beetle *(Meloe laevis)*
- ☐ Margined Burying Beetle *(Nicrophorus marginatus)*
- ☐ Metallic Wood-boring Beetles *(Buprestis spp.)*
- ☐ Nine-spotted Ladybug *(Coccinella novemnotata)*
- ☐ Pennsylvania Firefly or Woods Firefly *(Photuris pennsylvanicus)*
- ☐ Six-spotted Green Tiger Beetle *(Cicindela sexguttata)*
- ☐ Spotless "Nine-spotted" Ladybug *(Coccinella novemnotata franciscana)*
- ☐ Stag Beetle *(Pseudolucanus capreolus)*
- ☐ Two-spotted Ladybug *(Adalia bipunctata)*

Grasshoppers, Crickets and Cicadas:
- ☐ Annual or Dog-day Cicadas *(Tibicen spp.)*
- ☐ Angular-winged Katydid *(Microcentrum retinerve)*
- ☐ Black-horned Tree Cricket *(Oecanthus nigricornis)*
- ☐ Carolina Locust *(Dissosteira carolina)*
- ☐ Field Crickets *(Gryllus spp.)*
- ☐ Northern True Katydid *(Pterophylla camellifolia)*
- ☐ Periodical Cicadas *(Magicicada spp.)*
- ☐ Red-legged Grasshopper *(Melanoplus femurrubrum)*
- ☐ Snowy Tree Cricket *(Oecanthus fultoni)*

Mantids:
- ☐ Praying Mantis or European Mantid *(Mantis religiosa)*

Ants:
- ☐ Allegheny Mound Ant *(Formica exsectoides)*
- ☐ Black Carpenter Ant *(Camponotus pennsylvanicus)*

Lacewings:
- ☐ Green or Common Lacewings *(Chrysopa spp.)*

Dragonflies and Damselflies:

☐ Black-wing Damselfly or
Ebony Jewelwing *(Calopteryx maculata)*

☐ Civil Bluet Damselfly or
Familiar Bluet *(Enallagma civile)*

☐ Brown-spotted Yellow-wing Dragonfly or
Halloween Pennant *(Celithemis eponina)*

☐ Common Amberwing or
Eastern Amberwing Dragonfly *(Perithemis tenera)*

☐ Common Red Skimmer or
Ruby Meadowfly *(Sympetrum rubicundulum)*

☐ Elisa Skimmer or Calico Pennant *(Celithemis elisa)*

☐ Exclamation Forktail Damselfly or
Fragile Forktail Damselfly *(Ischnura posita)*

☐ Green Darner *(Anax junius)*

☐ Green-jacket Skimmer or
Eastern Pondhawk *(Erythemis simplicicollis)*

☐ Little Red Skimmer or
Yellow-legged Meadowfly *(Sympetrum vicinum)*

☐ Royal Skimmer or Prince Baskettail
(Epitheca princeps)

☐ Ten-spotted Dragonfly or
Twelve-spotted Skimmer *(Libellula pulchella)*

☐ Violet Dancer Damselfly *(Argia fumipennis)*

☐ White Tail Dragonfly or
Common Whitetail *(Libellula lydia)*

☐ Widow Skimmer *(Libellula luctuosa)*

Flies:

☐ Bee Flies *(Poecilanthrax spp.)*

☐ Black Flies *(Simulium spp.)*

☐ Blue Bottle Fly *(Calliphora vomitoria)*

☐ Crane Flies *(Tipula spp.)*

☐ Deer Flies *(Chrysops spp.)*

☐ Flood Plain Mosquito *(Aedes vexans)*

☐ Green Bottle Fly *(Phaenicia sericata)*

☐ Midges *(Chironomus spp.)*

☐ Robber Flies *(Promachus spp.)*

☐ Scorpionflies *(Panorpa spp.)*

Bees, Wasps, and Kin:

☐ Bald-faced Hornet *(Dolichovespula maculata)*

☐ Black-and-yellow Mud Dauber
(Sceliphron caementarium)

☐ Bumblebees *(Bombus spp.)*

☐ German Yellowjacket *(Vespula germanica)*

☐ Honeybee *(Apis mellifera)*

Moths:

☐ Gypsy Moth *(Lymantria dispar)*

☐ Hummingbird Moth *(Hemaris thysbe)*

☐ White-marked Tussock Moth *(Orgyia leucostigma)*

☐ Virginia Ctenuchid Moth *(Ctenucha virginica)*

Butterflies:

☐ Acadian Hairstreak Butterfly *(Satyrium acadicum)*

☐ American Copper Butterfly
(Lycaena phlaeas americana)

☐ Black Swallowtail Butterfly *(Papilio polyxenes)*

☐ Clouded Sulphur or
Common Sulphur *(Colias philodice)*

- [ ] Comma Butterfly (*Polygonia comma*)
- [ ] Common Wood Nymph Butterfly (*Cercyonis pegala alope*)
- [ ] Coral Hairstreak Butterfly (*Harkenclenus titus titus*)
- [ ] Delaware Skipper (*Atrytone logan*)
- [ ] Eastern Tailed Blue Butterfly (*Everes comyntas*)
- [ ] European Cabbage White Butterfly (*Pieris rapae*)
- [ ] European Skipper (*Thymelicus lineola*)
- [ ] Gray Hairstreak Butterfly (*Strymon melinus humuli*)
- [ ] Great Spangled Fritillary Butterfly (*Speyeria cybele*)
- [ ] Little Wood Satyr Butterfly (*Megisto cymela*)
- [ ] Monarch Butterfly (*Danaus plexippus plexippus*)
- [ ] Mourning Cloak Butterfly (*Nymphalis antiopa*)
- [ ] Orange Sulphur (*Colias eurytheme*)
- [ ] Painted Lady Butterfly (*Vanessa cardui*)
- [ ] Question Mark Butterfly (*Polygonia interrogationis*)
- [ ] Red Admiral Butterfly (*Vanessa atalanta rubria*)
- [ ] Red-spotted Purple Butterfly (*Limenitis arthemis astyanax*)
- [ ] Silver-spotted Skipper (*Epargyreus clarus*)
- [ ] Spicebush Swallowtail Butterfly (*Papilio troilus*)
- [ ] Spring Azure Butterfly (*Celastrina largiolus*)
- [ ] Tiger Swallowtail Butterfly (*Papilio glaucus*)
- [ ] Viceroy Butterfly (*Limenitus archippus*)

Reptiles

Snakes:
- [ ] Black Rat Snake (*Elaphe obsoleta*)
- [ ] Eastern Garter Snake (*Thamnophis sirtalis sirtalis*)
- [ ] Northern Brown Snake (*Storeria dekayi dekayi*)
- [ ] Northern Ringneck Snake (*Diadophis punctatus edwardsii*)
- [ ] Northern Watersnake (*Nerodia sipedon*)

Turtles:
- [ ] Common Snapping Turtle (*Chelydra serpentina*)
- [ ] Eastern Box Turtle (*Terrapene carolina*)
- [ ] Eastern Spiny Softshell Turtle (*Apalone spinifera spinifera*)
- [ ] Painted Turtle (*Chrysemys picta*)

Amphibians

Frogs:

- ☐ Bullfrog *(Rana catesbeiana)*
- ☐ Green Frog *(Rana clamitans)*
- ☐ Northern Leopard Frog *(Rana pipiens)*
- ☐ Pickerel Frog *(Rana palustris)*
- ☐ Western Chorus Frog *(Pseudacris triseriata triseriata)*
- ☐ Wood Frog *(Rana sylvatica)*

- ☐ Common Gray Treefrog *(Hyla versicolor)*
- ☐ Northern Spring Peeper *(Pseudacris crucifer crucifer)*

- ☐ American Toad *(Bufo americanus)*

- ☐ Red-spotted Newt *(Notophthalmus viridescens viridescens)*

Salamanders:

- ☐ Jefferson Salamander *(Ambystoma jeffersonianum)*
- ☐ Northern Dusky Salamander *(Desmognathus fuscus)*
- ☐ Northern Two-lined Salamander *(Eurycea bislineata)*
- ☐ Ravine Salamander *(Plethodon richmondi)*
- ☐ Red-backed Salamander *(Plethodon cinereus)*
- ☐ Spotted Salamander *(Ambystoma maculatum)*

Contributors & Acknowledgements

You have been introduced to the communities of plants and animals which make the Towpath Trail so interesting. Below is the community of individuals who contributed their diverse skills to the creation of this guide. We are grateful to them for their wealth of knowledge and hours of labor, but reserve to ourselves the responsibility for any errors of information presented in these pages.

The guide's natural resource committee:
Volunteers: Ann and Dwight Chasar, Mary Kay and Guy Newton (birds)
National Park Service staff: Paul H. Motts (amphibians, reptiles, insects), Meg Benke (mammals), Judy Knuth-Folts (flowers, trees), Dr. Tom Nash and Scott VanHouten (topography)

Other natural resource contributors:
Dr. Lowell P. Orr (amphibians, reptiles)
Dr. Sonja Teraguchi, Mike Greene, Bob Dispenza (insects)
Thomas Stanley (amphibians)
Dr. Tim Matson, Ralph Phingsten (amphibians)
Dr. Harold Marsh (winter)

National Park Service reviewers:
Barbara Pollarine, Diane Chalfant, Debbie Ayers
A special thanks to Ann and Dwight Chasar for their text describing bird activity, much of which was used verbatim. Also thanks to Jerry Welch for researching nature quotes and Leland Merk for typing the species lists.

Most of the illustrations were commissioned especially for this book. All works are copyrighted and used with permission.

Color photographs:
Ian Adams: pp. 9, 112.
Alice Phillips: amphibian icon.
Rob Bobel: pp. 17, 22, 48, 88, 94 (coltsfoot), 97, 101, 107, 108 (stump).
Tom Cawley: reptile icon, winter icon, pp. 35, 50, 67, 85, 100, 122, 136.
Tom Jones: cover, tree icon, pp. 14-15, 26-27, 56-57, 92, 108-109, 132.
Jim Roetzel: bird icon, flower icon, mammal icon, insect icon, pp. 18, 30, 31, 42, 43, 46, 63, 65, 75, 78, 79, 82, 94 (forget-me-nots), 95, 113, 114, 117, 118, 121, 123, 128, 129, 130, 131,134.

Jef Sturm, pp. 10, 138.
National Park Service: p. 3, topography icon.
Black and white photographs:
National Park Service: pp. 103, 107.
National Park Service historic archives: pp. 5, 14, 25, 38, 39, 5, 73, 74, 127.

Illustrations:
Rob Bobel: pp. 15, 49(frog), 61, 66 (turtle), 87, 93, 99, 116, 132
Ed Calmer: pp. 33, 97.
Claudia James: pp. 20-21, 40-41, 76-77.
Kim Norley: pp. 52, 69 (creek section), 104.
Reni Pavia: pp. 45 (bur oak), 47 (butterfly), 66 (mantis).
Arrye Rosser: pp. 36, 47(vole), 49 (turtle), 62, 98, 119, 123, 130
Robert Tubbesing: pp. 16, 19, 28-29, 31, 32, 33 (butterfly), 44, 45 (buckeye), 48, 51, 58-59, 64, 68, 69 (tracks), 70, 80, 81, 82, 83, 84, 96, 102, 110-111, 115, 131, 133, 134, 137.
Jef Sturm Graphic Design: p. 17.
Towpath maps drawn by Kim Norley and adapted by Jef Sturm Graphic Design
Chapter title pages from photographs by Tom Jones and adapted by Jef Sturm Graphic Design

The authors, Peg and Rob Bobel, were founding members of the Cuyahoga Valley Trails Council. They edited the Trails Council's earlier works, the first and second editions of the *Trail Guide Handbook, Cuyahoga Valley National Recreation Area*. For *The Nature of the Towpath,* Peg wrote the text and Rob was responsible for design, layout, and production.

Peg is the Executive Director of the Cuyahoga Valley Association, the park's friends group. Rob is a civil engineer for the park and is actively involved in the development of the Ohio & Erie Canal National Heritage Corridor.

The Cuyahoga Valley Trails Council, Inc. is a not-for-profit, all-volunteer organization dedicated to building and maintaining trails in the Cuyahoga Valley. The Trails Council conducts monthly volunteer trail work projects and publishes trail books.

For more information or to receive their quarterly newsletter, *The Cuyahoga Valley Explorer*, write: Cuyahoga Valley Trails Council, Inc., 810 Cedar Grove Circle, Sagamore Hills, OH 44067.

All publication proceeds are used for trail or trail related projects within CVNRA.

The Nature of the Towpath was designed and typeset by Jef Sturm Graphic Design, Pawleys Island, South Carolina. The book type face is Minion and Handwriting.

The book was printed by Franklin Printing Company, Inc., Akron, Ohio and was bound at Steffen Bookbinders in Macedonia, Ohio. The paper is Mohawk 50/10 white matte 100 pound text which contains a minimum of 15% post-consumer waste fiber.

The authors used numerous field guides in putting this book together. They particularly recommend the Peterson Field Guide Series, the Audubon Society Field Guides, and the Stokes Nature Guides. Other excellent sources of natural history information, especially for younger or beginning naturalists, include Peterson First Guide Series, CVNRA ranger-led programs and the Discovery Packs (see page 8).

Notes